Mayer Matalon

Mayer Matalon

Business, Politics and the Jewish-Jamaican Elite

Diana Thorburn

HAMILTON BOOKS
Lanham • Boulder • New York • London

Published by Hamilton Books
An imprint of The Rowman & Littlefield Publishing Group, Inc.
4501 Forbes Boulevard, Suite 200, Lanham, Maryland 20706
www.rowman.com

6 Tinworth Street, London SE11 5AL, United Kingdom

Copyright © 2019 The Rowman & Littlefield Publishing Group, Inc.

All rights reserved. No part of this book may be reproduced in any form or by any electronic or mechanical means, including information storage and retrieval systems, without written permission from the publisher, except by a reviewer who may quote passages in a review.

British Library Cataloguing in Publication Information Available

Library of Congress Cataloging-in-Publication Data Available

ISBN 9780761871149 (pbk.)
ISBN 9780761871156 (electronic)

For Wayne.

Contents

List of Figures		ix
Acknowledgments		xi
Introduction		xiii
1	Landmarks	1
2	Beginnings	9
3	Early Years in Business	23
4	The Numbers Man	43
5	The Growth of ICD	49
6	Housing	59
7	On the Inside of Political Decision Making, 1950–2010	69
8	Jamaica's Chairman of the Board: Bank of Nova Scotia and Cable and Wireless	89
9	The End of an Era	99
10	The World of Mayer Matalon	107
Postscript		117
Sources		119
Appendix: Further Reading		121

Bibliography	123
Index	129
About the Author	137

List of Figures

Figure 1.1	Mayer Matalon receiving the Order of Jamaica, Jamaica's highest national honor, in recognition of his service to the nation, with particular reference to his leadership in the bauxite negotiations, from Governor General Sir Florizel Glasspole, October, 1976. Photo courtesy of Joseph M. Matalon.	2
Figure 2.1	Mayer as a baby, 1922. Photo courtesy of Joseph M. Matalon.	17
Figure 3.1	Mayer with his boss in the US Base Authorities Panama Canal Zone, around 1943. Photo courtesy of Joseph M. Matalon.	24
Figure 3.2	Mayer and Sarita's wedding party, March 31, 1949 wedding. L-R, Pauline Goodman (sister), Abraham Shalom (Felix Shalom's father), Florizel Matalon (mother), Estelle Shalom (Sarita's sister), Mayer, Sarita, Eli (brother), Rebeca Castell (Sarita's mother), Aaron (Mayer's brother), Felix Shalom (Sarita's brother-in-law). Photo courtesy of Joseph M. Matalon.	35
Figure 3.3	Sarita and Mayer on the occasion of their daughter Diana's wedding, London, 1966. Photo courtesy of Joseph M. Matalon.	37
Figure 4.1	Mayer Matalon (right), leading his horse back to the stables at Caymanas Park on March 13, 1967. Courtesy of the Gleaner Company (Media) Limited.	44

List of Figures

Figure 5.1	Mayer with his mother and siblings at her birthday celebration, 1970. L-R back row, Owen, Mayer, Vernon, Eli, Aaron, Zackie, Moses L-R front row, Gloria, Florizel, Pauline, Adele, Photo courtesy of Joseph M. Matalon.	51
Figure 6.1	Image that appeared of Mayer Matalon in LIFE magazine. The original caption was "Jamaican builder Mayer Matalon talking with a tenant of a typical new house." April 01, 1959. Robert W. Kelley | The LIFE Picture Collection | Getty Images.	60
Figure 6.2	Independence City housing scheme construction site, March 9, 1968. The Prime Minister, the Hon. Hugh Shearer (second, left) talks with Mayer Matalon, in his capacity as chairman of West Indies Home Contractors. Others in the group (from left, front) are: the Hon. Wilton Hill, Minister of Housing; the Hon. Victor Grant, Minister of Legal Affairs (M.P. for the Area); Mr. Warren Wolff, A. I. D. investment officer; Mr. Lloyd Collins, Permanent Secretary, Ministry of Housing. At the rear are Mr. Richard Ware, head of A. I. D. in Jamaica; Mr. Walter Tobriner, American Ambassador; and Mr. Robert Montgomery, managing director of Jamaica National Mortgage Association Ltd., developers of the scheme. Courtesy of the Gleaner Company (Media) Limited	62
Figure 8.1	Mayer Matalon, in his capacity as chairman, carrying out the ceremonial listing of Telecommunications of Jamaica (TOJ) on the Jamaica Stock Exchange, October 27, 1988. Courtesy of the Gleaner Company (Media) Limited	92
Figure 9.1	Mayer with his son Joe M., early 2000s, Photo courtesy of Joseph M. Matalon.	103

Acknowledgments

I am grateful to my husband Wayne Chen, who encouraged me to explore my own nagging questions about business and politics in Jamaica by writing this book. Once the idea was concrete, so many people encouraged me but chief among them was R. Danny Williams, to whom I owe immense gratitude for his support and patience. Ainsley Henriques's assistance and encouragement throughout was invaluable. I had the blessing and input of Mayer Matalon's children Joe M., Jacqueline, Gail and Rebeca. I am humbled by the trust they placed in me to tell their father's story while having no editorial control over what I wrote. O. K. Melhado and Pat Rousseau read several drafts and gave valuable comments; their assurances that I had "gotten Mayer right" emboldened me to press on. My friend, Farrah Brown, reviewed many drafts and gave me an objective reader's perspective, which I greatly appreciated. Matthew J. Smith guided me on critical aspects of the research and publication process. Lisa Vasciannie lent moral and logistical support at crucial stages. I appreciate the kindness that so many people extended to me by granting me interviews, and their openness to sharing so much with me. Many other friends and acquaintances helped with small actions and gestures such as checking a fact, reading a paragraph for accuracy, lending me an out-of-print magazine with an essential article, offering an anecdote, helping to arrange an interview, or simply having a conversation with me about something in the book that they had knowledge of, and, in so doing, deepened my own understanding of the material.

Sagicor, the Bank of Nova Scotia, and Myers, Fletcher and Gordon gave financial support that made the writing of the book possible. The CHASE

Fund supported the book's production. The Private Sector Organization of Jamaica endorsed the project and provided institutional support.

To all of the above-mentioned, and those who are not named: a huge, everlasting thank you. Without you this book would not be.

Introduction

The whale only gets harpooned when he comes up to spout.[1]

Mayer Michael Matalon is a legend in Jamaican business and politics. From the 1950s through to the 1990s he was perhaps the single most influential individual, outside of politics, in twentieth-century Jamaica. Known as "Jamaica's Chairman of the Board,"[2] and "The Triple M,"[3] Mayer Matalon made the Matalon name synonymous with wealth, power and innovation in Jamaica. He played a lead role in his family's rise in business from the late-1940s through the 1980s, particularly his family business's pioneering endeavors in housing and infrastructure developments from the 1960s onwards.

His position in the inner circle of Norman Manley's People's National Party, his close relationship with Michael Manley throughout the 1990s, and his influential relationships with JLP leaders, together with his connections in international business and finance, which he leveraged with his relationships in the Jamaican government, made Mayer Matalon the quintessential power broker. He knew that true power lay in the ability to call the prime minister on a direct line and have his call taken right away, and he enjoyed that power for some forty years. However, he had no interest in broadcasting his influence and relationships, which he guarded with extreme discretion.

Mayer Matalon was distinguished by the fact that he cared, not only about the profit margin of his businesses, but about their national impact, which led him to seek opportunities beyond mere commerce and self-interest. As a result, he is considered by Jamaicans and others who worked with him or witnessed his life over half a century, whether up close or from afar, to be the epitome of what, in the twenty-first century, we call the social entrepreneur.

Mayer Matalon and his siblings are not the only entrepreneurial family of their era—1950s–1990s—to fit that description, but they are the most prominent. The question is why? What was it about Mayer and his brothers' background and upbringing, about the family as a whole, that made them so remarkable? What enabled them to bring together the spirit of enterprise and national development in the Jamaican context? What can we learn from their story?

Mayer Matalon was a public figure, but he did not seek the limelight. He avoided publicity as best he could and never enjoyed having a TV camera pointed at him. Many of his brothers were more comfortable in the public eye, and he was often able to deflect attention onto them. Being widely recognized had no value to him; being recognized by powerful people did. He often cautioned others about the proverbial whale which only got caught when coming up to spout; in essence his philosophy was to get on with the work without making a noise about it.

Aside from his mathematical genius, connections to power, negotiating skills and visionary business acumen, Mayer Matalon is known, among all who were acquainted with him, for his wit, humor and love of teasing—he only teased people that he was fond of; those he didn't tease he didn't hold in much regard—which he did so cleverly that they were never offended. He was fond of using droll aphorisms, sometimes so outré that they would be considered extremely politically incorrect in 2019. His ability to connect with people from all walks of life, and to make them feel that he was really listening to them, endeared him to virtually all who crossed his path.

In this account of his life I tell the story of an innovative, hardworking Jamaican, a businessman, and a public servant: how Mayer Matalon came to be that person, and how he made his way. The original title of this book, *The Baron*, was a nickname given to him by his brothers, a name they called with fondness. It was a moniker that he relished, earned by his success in a notable negotiation. When he arranged for Eagle Star Insurance Company to provide the mortgages for the Mona housing development, it was the first in a series of housing innovations that had never been seen before in Jamaica. The nickname and its origins speak to the importance of Mayer's family in his rise to prominence. The closeness of the eleven siblings as a family unit played an important role in laying the foundation of the growing economic and social power from which they all benefitted. The nickname "the Baron" embodies a persona of consequence and connections, in an era when an individual could wield significant political influence in a small newly-independent country like Jamaica.

Among the innumerable honors Mayer Matalon received in his lifetime was the highest that Jamaica bestows on its outstanding citizens, the Order of Jamaica. But he left no papers, no letters, no diaries. He seldom granted interviews. He refused multiple attempts by the wife of one of his closest friends, the author of published biographies, to interview him for a book such as this one. His children encouraged him to make notes toward a book, but, as often happens with people who have lived remarkable lives, he never did.

Jamaica is unlikely ever to witness another such individual, not only because Mayer Matalon was unique in the particular mix of intellect, wit, proficiency with numbers, negotiating skills, understanding of relationships, and political savvy that made him a trailblazer, but because Jamaica and the world have changed. May this account stand as a record of the time, the place, and the man.

NOTES

1. Mayer was well known for this aphorism; its original source is unknown.
2. Gordon Robinson, "Mayer Matalon—Jamaica's 'Chairman of the Board,'" *Gleaner*, July 22, 2012.
3. Edward Baugh, *Chancellor, I Present: A Collection of Convocation Citations Given at the University of the West Indies, Mona 1985–1998* (Kingston: University of the West Indies Press, 2000), 1–24.

Chapter One

Landmarks

Mayer Matalon died on February 3, 2012, one month shy of his ninetieth birthday. The landmarks of a full and distinguished career had begun when he was just a boy in the early 1930s, when he was awarded a scholarship to one of the island's most elite schools, Jamaica College (JC). In the immediate post-World War II period, as a young man in his midtwenties, he embarked on his business career and his role as advisor to Jamaica's political leaders.

His initial position was as founder, director, chairman and *de facto* chief financial officer of his family's businesses. He went on to hold chairmanships and directorships of multiple public and private entities, to serve as an official and unofficial advisor to premiers, prime ministers and ministers of finance from the days of Norman Manley in the 1940s through to the government of Bruce Golding in 2011, and he actively participated, usually in a leadership position, in a wide variety of civic organizations. As a visionary and an innovator he brought pioneering ideas to Jamaica, which he implemented both publicly, in his own businesses, and behind the scenes, in government policy formulation and implementation.

He was, for example, a director of the United Congregation of Israelites and chair of the board of his alma mater, Jamaica College. He led the Jamaican government's negotiations, in what was arguably the most extensive and important foreign negotiation that Jamaica has ever undertaken, over bauxite in 1974. He held the office of deputy chairman, and in most people's view, *de facto* chairman, of the Bank of Nova Scotia Jamaica, the largest and most profitable private bank in Jamaica, for forty-five years. He chaired the state-owned Jamaica Telephone Company through to its twenty-plus year transformation and privatization to Cable and Wireless Jamaica, and then chaired C&W Jamaica to record profits as a private entity. He was passionate about and owned many racehorses and, for some years, a stud farm. He was honorary consul for Sweden.

In his personal life, he was a devoted husband for sixty-three years, a family man and father of five. His son, Joseph Mayer, the only one of his offspring who remained in Jamaica, has followed in his father's footsteps in business and public service.

In the Jamaican context, there is no meaningful honor or accolade that was not conferred on Mayer Matalon. Among the many awards he received throughout his long life three stand out for their prestige, and from these and their citations we can begin to understand the extent of his contribution to Jamaica and how it was perceived.

In 1976 he was awarded the Order of Jamaica (fig. 1.1), the nation's highest honor, for his contributions to nation building, specifically his role in the bauxite levy negotiations.

Figure 1.1. Mayer Matalon receiving the Order of Jamaica, Jamaica's highest national honor, in recognition of his service to the nation, with particular reference to his leadership in the bauxite negotiations, from Governor General Sir Florizel Glasspole, October, 1976.
Photo courtesy of Joseph M. Matalon.

In 1994 the Private Sector Organization of Jamaica (PSOJ) inducted him into their Hall of Fame. In addition to recognizing the accomplishments that the government had celebrated nearly twenty years earlier, the citation described him as:

> [A] brilliant financier and negotiator.... The many successes of his career... [are] due to his diligence, keen intellect, tenacity, high sense of integrity, sharp business acumen and keen entrepreneurial instincts. Mayer Matalon has successfully negotiated several key deals for the family-owned operation and has a proud record in his position as Industrial Commercial Development's—known better as ICD—first and only Chairman. His negotiating skills came to the fore in the family's entry into housing as he arranged the financing for Jamaica's first mass housing project at Mona.
>
> This formed an excellent foundation for the historic achievements of West Indies Home Contractors Limited, where over 24,000 units have been built in thirty years, housing more than 100,000 Jamaicans. The company, chaired by Mayer Matalon, is now involved in the single largest housing project in the Caribbean region, The Greater Portmore Housing Project which on completion will feature 10,000 units housing in excess of 50,000 people.[1]

In 1996, when an honorary doctorate was conferred on him by the University of the West Indies, Mona, the citation declared:

> He believed, with humility, that he was blessed with "a feel for money." This gift, coupled with an equally brilliant gift for negotiation, has been the dynamic of his success.
>
> His captaincy made the ICD Group a model and genial giant in the world of private enterprise. The ICD Group has made sterling contributions in industry, commerce and development, not only to the benefit of the Matalon family, but to the well-being of society as a whole.
>
> Mona Heights, Harbour View, Duhaney Park, Portmore and Greater Portmore: the scale and timeliness of these projects bear witness to a truly creative and sheltering vision.
>
> His willingness to serve his country has been matched by his material generosity [which the UWI Mona campus benefited from in multiple arenas]. The university benefited for years from his financial acumen, through his being a member of its Investments Committee.
>
> He has been dignified by the reason and equanimity with which he has met criticism and challenges.
>
> We may conclude that the triple-M signifies merit, magnanimity and munificence.[2]

At his memorial service, tributes were read by Omar Davies, PNP member of Parliament and former minister of finance, Pat Rousseau, his friend, lawyer, and racehorse co-owner of over fifty years, and his son, Joseph. Davies spoke of Mayer Matalon's extensive public service:

> During the 1970s, Mayer headed the team which negotiated, on behalf of Jamaica, to increase the country's take from the bauxite/alumina sector. Apart from the financial benefits to the country, I believe that the work of that team did much to increase national self-confidence, by demonstrating that a group of Jamaicans was capable of matching negotiating skills with the high-priced financial and legal experts assembled by the companies.
>
> While Mayer was never a card-carrying PNP supporter, his close association with Michael Manley was well known. In the 1980s Michael Manley sought to reassess the policies and programs implemented during the 70s in an attempt to determine the factors which had led to the massive electoral defeat. He sought Mayer's responses not only because they were personal friends, not only because of his fine business mind, but moreso because he felt that he would present to him an honest appraisal free from the window dressing which often characterizes views being presented to a political leader.
>
> There are several areas where there were fundamental changes in the PNP's policies, having regained office in 1989. The period in opposition, constructively utilized, had served its purpose well. Mayer contributed to this rethinking, as public service within our democratic tradition.
>
> In the new PNP administration of 1989, Manley appointed Mayer to his Council of Economic Advisors. The council had many discussions concerning the liberalization of the foreign exchange system, one of the most significant economic decisions taken in Jamaica's fifty-year history as an independent country.
>
> When I was appointed Minister of Finance in 1993 by Prime Minister P.J. Patterson, he advised me to meet with the major figures in the domestic private sector in order to determine their main issues of concern, as well as the ways in which we could foster an improved relationship between business and the Administration. In following that advice, I began meeting with Mayer on a regular basis.
>
> We do not have the time to discuss all the issues where I sought, and received, advice from Mayer. To be truthful, there are several instances where I still do not feel at liberty to fully reveal the challenges faced and the advice and solutions which he offered. However, I will share two examples of the support provided to me and to the Government during that period.
>
> The first relates to the crisis in the financial sector which first appeared in the mid-1990s. Mayer's observations and intuitive analysis were borne out by the work of the forensic auditors as we uncovered numerous irregularities [which precipitated the crisis] in several of the financial groups.
>
> The second example took place in December 2003 when revenues for the fiscal year fell dramatically below the amounts we had projected. Our problem

was acute as the domestic creditors, being aware of the crisis, had shown no inclination to acquire new GOJ paper. Then-Financial Secretary Shirley Tyndall came to me, late on a Tuesday afternoon in mid-December, to indicate that we faced a challenge in meeting obligations for the end of the month saying, "No Administration can survive if it cannot make its pay bill at Christmas." We tossed around ideas for several hours and came up with no viable solution. Late in the evening Shirley finally suggested, "Why don't you call Mayer and see what ideas he has?" This I did.

Mayer said, "Papa, this is bigger than me." He concluded that we needed external help. On Wednesday he called me back to ask me whether I would be free to travel on the Thursday because he had got an appointment for me with the Chairman of a major North American bank on Friday. On Thursday the Financial Secretary, the BOJ Governor and I were on a flight to keep our Friday appointment. After several hours of intense grilling, the Chairman [of the major North American bank] took the decision, against the advice of his deputies, and without going to his board, to grant us a special loan.

We took the flight out back to Jamaica on Saturday which allowed payment of the Government's obligations for December. All this had been accomplished with only Prime Minister Patterson being aware of the extent of the crisis and only a few persons knowing how we had engineered our way out of it. I cannot think of any other person at that stage, with the international contacts and influence, to have facilitated that meeting with a major international bank's Chairman with just one day's notice.[3]

Pat Rousseau paid tribute to the man he had known since he (Mayer) was in his thirties:

In his head was a brilliant mind and he could only be described as possessing special qualities that are near genius. His exceptional skill as a mathematician, his capacity to assess any situation successfully and his prodigious memory, coupled with a great sense of humor, made him wonderful company whether in his office, at the negotiation table, at the Race Track or in the comfort of his home.

Calculators were not allowed in his office because he said they made for a lazy mind. You were encouraged to use your mental skills or resort to calculating on paper. I saw more than one calculator hit the wall in those early days as Mayer enforced the rule with all his managers. Mayer could multiply and divide four digit numbers mentally quicker than you could do it on a calculator. It was an amazing skill. I saw him win many a bet with his managers.

Mayer employed these skills at the racetrack in his assessment of horses. He always argued that Caymanas was the perfect situation for applying a mathematical system to analyze performance because the conditions rarely changed.

His analytical powers in financial and other matters were astounding. With no formal tertiary education he was equal to the best financial analysts you could bring before him.

Mayer was a fascinating, larger than life character of great integrity and an excellent negotiator. I saw these skills employed in Caracas, Trinidad, New York, Washington, London, Sierra Leone, Nigeria and Jamaica with great success. He always wanted to be a lawyer and developed very good skills as a cross-examiner as he showed in the formal hearings in the bauxite negotiations.[4]

And from Joe, his devoted son:

[He was a] committed husband, utterly besotted by his wife of over sixty years, and devoted to his children, grand- and great-grandchildren, all of whom gave him the greatest joy.

Far beyond the circles of family I am constantly in wonder of the number of persons whose lives he touched in positive ways. The turnout here today, by Jamaicans from all walks of life, bears testament to that fact.

I had the privilege also of working closely with him for twenty-five years and could never have wished for a more brilliant and dynamic mentor and teacher, whose vision and foresight are unparalleled in my experience. My closest friend, he taught me perhaps the most important of lessons: that a man's word is his bond and that one should always stand firmly on principle, no matter the consequence.

Although he never attended university, Mayer was a natural scholar and one of the most widely read people I have ever met. Perhaps his favorite literary form was poetry, and he would often quote verse to us at length and entirely from memory.

Mayer had an abiding love for and commitment to his country, and in the almost ninety years of his life that love and commitment never once faltered. I recall during the late 1970s when a friend jokingly asked whether he would be the last to turn out the lights, his great and ever-present sense of humor moved him to quip, "Don't worry about me, I will be here to supervise the person turning out the lights."[5]

These excerpts set the stage for the rest of the story: how Mayer Matalon came to be who he was, and to do all he did. For those who did not bear witness to the public aspects of Mayer Matalon's life—and much of it was public because his work, whether in private business or public service, was inextricably tied up with the nation's interests—let the story contained in these pages act as introduction to one of the foremost personalities of Jamaica's postwar, postindependence development.

NOTES

1. Private Sector Organization of Jamaica, citation to Mayer Matalon on his admission to the PSOJ Hall of Fame, 1994.

2. Edward Baugh, *Chancellor, I Present: A Collection of Convocation Citations Given at the University of the West Indies, Mona 1985–1998* (Kingston: University of the West Indies Press, 2000), 1–24.

3. Omar Davies, "Tribute to Mayer Matalon," eulogy for Mayer Matalon, Shaare Shalom Synagogue, Kingston, Jamaica, February 7, 2012.

4. Pat Rousseau, "Tribute," eulogy for Mayer Matalon, Shaare Shalom Synagogue, Kingston, Jamaica, February 7, 2012.

5. Joseph M. Matalon, "Remembrances of Dad," eulogy for Mayer Matalon, Shaare Shalom Synagogue, Kingston, Jamaica, February 7, 2012.

Chapter Two

Beginnings

KINGSTON DOCKS, 1910

Stepping onto the dock, Joseph scanned the crowd for his brother. He wasn't hard to spot, despite his skin being a few shades darker than when he last saw him, after ten years' exposure to the Jamaican sun. Yet Moses Matalon was still among the palest faces in the throng when he disembarked from the *Hamburg* that bright morning in Kingston.

Moses pushed forward to his brother, greeting him in Arabic. What a comfort to hear familiar words after so many weeks at sea! Joseph had studied English as a young man, but it had been many years ago, back in Damascus, and after ten years in Mexico, it was rusty. Even so, the chatter among the people that he was now hearing around him sounded like another language entirely, nothing like the English he knew.

Joseph had made it, at last, to Jamaica. What he was coming to he had little idea, but no matter, he didn't intend to stay; his intention was to catch up with Moses and then get back on the *Hamburg* and continue to Cuba,[1] where a sister and her sons were, among the over five thousand Damascus Sephardim who had settled there since the 1900s.[2] Or perhaps on to Panama, where other siblings and cousins had settled. Surely he would have better luck in one of those places than he had had in Mexico.

Damascus, from where Moses, Joseph, and many other Jews who were now sprinkled throughout the Americas had come, was the past, never to be returned to. In the midst of political, social and economic instability, and the targeted persecution of Jews who had lost the protection that they had enjoyed for centuries under Ottoman rule,[3] Joseph, even as a teenager, had known that he would have to leave. There was no future for him there.

The inevitability of fleeing Damascus was borne in on him by the droves of people who were leaving. Every day, more houses were abandoned by their owners. Furniture, clothes, even food were left behind, though never for very long as they would be salvaged and picked through within a few days. The villages grew emptier, quieter, more deserted; the sense of despair ballooned to fill the vacuum where once children played, commerce thrived and people lived their lives.

But it took a lot to leave, including a way out. The arrival of the railroad in Damascus in 1894 provided a path,[4] and Joseph made his way to Jerusalem. Unable to continue the rabbinical studies that he had embarked on in Damascus, he learned the textile trade.[5] It wasn't until 1899 that he and other family members finally got it all together—the money, the will, the fortitude—to actually make the journey. He was twenty-four years old.

Not all of Joseph's family came to the Americas. Some remained in the region, moving around to safer places on foot, to more stable towns and villages in Beirut and what is today Israel. The sister in Havana eventually returned to Israel with her children. But the whole family scattered, and were dislocated from their place of origin, as were many hundreds of thousands of their countrymen.

Migration out of the Levant began in the 1860s and picked up in the 1890s. Hundreds of thousands of people emigrated from what are today Lebanon, Syria and Palestine, following the collapse of the Turkish Ottoman Empire in the second half of the nineteenth century,[6] in a way not dissimilar to the Syrian exodus that the world witnessed from 2014. There was a great deal of unrest, often manifesting in violent conflicts between different ethnic and religious groups. The Middle Eastern exodus of 1880 to 1920, which dispersed the Levantine Jews throughout the New World, was the wave of emigration that brought the "Syrians" to the Caribbean—the Mahfoods, the Ammars, the Issas, the Sabgas, and the forebears of Edward Seaga, who became Jamaica's prime minister in 1980.[7] And the Matalons.

Unlike the mostly Maronite Christians and Druze who arrived in the Caribbean from the Levant, of the Sephardim Jews who had left the Levant in their tens of thousands, very few came to the English-speaking Caribbean. Many more Jews went north to the United States, and to South and Central America.[8] Moses and Joseph were two of a handful who came to Jamaica; the Settons, the Shaloms, the Dowecks, and a few others. The historical record has largely missed them, or they missed the record, as they have stayed off the radar. All eventually moved on from Jamaica to other places, if not within a few years of arriving in Jamaica, then in the 1970s.

Joseph had intended to go the United States, but ended up in Mexico, where he tried to establish himself. Why he left Mexico is unknown, but he may have been driven out by the uncertainty brought on by the Mexican Revolution. Having known and endured political instability in Damascus, and having fled it once already, Joseph would not have wanted to go through it again.

Moses convinced Joseph to stay, telling him: "Jamaica is a very nice place. British government, law and order and discipline, with a Jewish community. Why don't you spend some time?"[9] But the Jamaica that Joseph met in 1910 was a society in flux, where colonial strictures on race and color were being challenged and reshaped, where the socioeconomic hierarchy of a white and near-white elite, including some Jamaican Jews, atop a black majority, was being penetrated by a small number of educated black and brown Jamaicans, and where the seeds of the labor riots of the 1930s were beginning to be planted.[10] Though he may not have been able to intuit it from the alien culture and surroundings, Joseph was about to witness, and in some small way participate in, what would amount to a massive sea change in Jamaican politics and society. A sea change in which his offspring would be inextricably involved.

KINGSTON, 7 JANUARY 1914

He was more than twice her age, but Florizel Madge Henriques knew that a marriage opportunity like this would not likely come her way again. A white man, a Jew, was to be her husband. So what if he was a foreigner? He spoke English and French and Spanish and Arabic. And in order to survive he had picked up some Jamaican in the four years he had been on the island. It was essential in the dry goods trade that he had engaged in with his brother, first in St. Thomas and then in Kingston, for the previous three years.

The "Syrians"—whether Maronite Christians, Druze or the recently arrived Jews—had disrupted the dry goods market since they came to Jamaica. It wasn't glamorous work. They were peddlers, hucksters, hawkers, considered by the colonial gentry almost on the same level as beggars.[11] Their pursuits and successes further destabilized a status quo that was in flux, already being contested from many angles. These brash new merchants removed the austere, intimidating barrier between supplier and consumer by going straight to the customer, often on a buggy, on mule, or by foot. No longer did a person of color, or of modest means, have to steel him- or herself to enter an establishment manned by British colonials or their descendants, where he would be treated with disdain at worst, indifference at best, in order to do their business. Thanks to the Syrian traders, they no longer had to already know what they wanted to buy before entering the premises, and meekly ask to see it from behind the counter. No more did the seamstress, or tailor, or small retailer have to summon his or her best English to try to sound respectable enough to make a purchase. The ordinary person now had access to fabrics and trimmings with which they too could make their own fashionable clothes, whether for themselves or for a customer. They now had information on what was available and they could exercise options. They were part of an emerging middle class—of sorts—and could now dress the part.

The Syrians learned the Jamaican dialect, or their best approximation. They were friendly. They didn't discriminate. They showed you all the goods they had. They remembered what you liked and took from the bottom of their basket the item they had brought just for you. They gave credit. They were interested in making the sale. The old English way of doing things couldn't survive, and it did not. The Arabs soon monopolized commerce, at the same time as agriculture and landholding were beginning to lose their foothold as sources of wealth and power.[12]

This is where Joseph Matalon found his base, among Jamaica's new merchant class. It didn't matter that he was one of very few Jews among the Levantines who had come to Jamaica, he was considered a "Syrian" in the Jamaican context. Despite their different religions, they shared a common sensibility and approach toward this type of work.[13]

Never did Florizel think such a being would come into her world, creating the possibility that she would be the wife of a white foreigner. She didn't even know where Damascus was, or Mexico, before he showed her in an atlas book. He had been to more places in Jamaica in the few years he had been on the island than she had in her entire fifteen years of life. He said he would show her how to be a Jew. She figuratively nodded assent, not knowing what that meant, except that she had always been a Jew and it had had no discernible effect on her life up to that point.

Joseph had never expected this either. When he had left Mexico he was already in his mid-thirties. In the decade he had been there he had not found a wife among the other Jewish migrants, nor among the Mexicans.[14] Perhaps, he had thought, he would have better chances in Cuba, or in Panama, where there was a larger pool of Levantine Jews.[15] On arriving in Jamaica, it didn't even enter his mind that a wife and a family might be among his prospects, that he might start a whole new life here.

But here she was, fifteen years old, a rare, uncut gem. By the time he met her he had learned enough Jamaican English that he could understand her and she him. She was from a poor, uneducated family, but she was Jewish and she was beautiful. They each considered themselves the lucky one. By coincidence, their fathers were both named Isaac, so of course their first son would be named Isaac too. And so he was, born their second child in 1916, a year after Pauline, their first-born.

Such an unlikely pair—how did they even find each other? They met in Chapelton.[16] It is said that they were introduced by a Palestinian Jew, Shamas, who stocked the dry goods store that Moses was running, and where Joseph was working.[17] Perhaps Shamas saw the mutual benefit that they would bring to each other, despite her being so young and him being so much older. After all, the twenty-four-year age difference was hardly remarkable in the early 1900s.

Florizel was one of thirteen children. Her mother Hannah, née Vaz, was a Jamaican Jewess. Her father was a Henriques, one of three Isaac Henriques born around the same time. They were the descendants of the Jamaican Jews who could trace their heritage on the island back hundreds of years, from the arrival of the "Portugals," Portuguese-Spanish Jewish *conversos* or *Marranos* fleeing the Inquisition in the late 1500s to Amsterdam and on to Jamaica. (Jews were not allowed to openly practice Judaism in Jamaica until after the English capture of the island in 1655.) Ensuing waves of Jewish immigrants to Jamaica resulted and by the mid-1800s, with legislation allowing them full citizenship in 1831–1832, they became a prosperous and politically influential group.[18] By 1849 eight of the forty-seven members of Jamaica's House of Assembly were Jewish and the Assembly closed on the Jewish Day of Atonement, Yom Kippur, because so many members were attending synagogue services.[19]

But Isaac and Hannah were not among the establishment Jews, the ones the historians and academics have written about—the Ashenheims and DeCordovas and DeLissers. These and other renowned Jamaican Jews were prosperous merchants in the 1700s, but according to a slave society status quo, were considered second-class citizens because of their religion. The color of their skin meant they ranked above the enslaved and the free colored, but they were not allowed to vote until a few decades into the 1800s. After the Haitian Revolution the British colonialists realized that they, as a tiny minority of the island's population, needed all the whites on their side, and put anti-Semitism aside to elevate the Jamaican Jews to "full white" status. Many of these financially successful Jews then went on to become prominent and influential as politicians, lawyers and newspapermen.

Florizel and her dozen siblings were Jewish, but they were not wealthy, or accomplished, or well-known. Florizel's mother earned her living from a stall in the Coronation Market. Florizel and her family would not even have been known to the establishment Jews. There were so many Jews in Jamaica—in 1881, some two thousand five hundred—that they didn't all know each other, even if they shared the same last name. Furthermore, Florizel's family were "lesser" Henriques—"nobody Jews" in the exact words that elite Jews of that era used to refer to them.[20] (They were also called "herring Jews" a somewhat contemptuous reference to their occupation as small shopkeepers.)[21] And there were more than a few of them; they just haven't been written about and are not present in the historical record of Jamaica's Jews.

But poor Jamaican Jews there were: the Hebrew Benevolent Society was established in 1851 to alleviate the distress "prevailing among the Jewish poor" after the 1850 cholera outbreak. It continued as an almshouse, changing its name to The Jewish Home in 1911.[22] Until the mid-1900s it took in mostly poor aged Jews and Jewish foundlings.

Jews like Florizel and her family didn't go to synagogue, even while those Jamaican Jews who did attend synagogue may not themselves have been particularly devout. They intermarried with "ordinary" Jamaicans, dispersed their whiteness and lost their religion. These were the Jews who left behind the trail of black and brown Jamaicans with Jewish names—Cohen and Levy and Lindo and Bravo—many of whom, within a generation, had no notion of their Jewishness. Jews who, at the founding of Israel in 1948 would likely not have heard the news, and if they had, would probably have had no inkling that it had anything to do with them. Florizel and her kin's whiteness may have given them some elevated status, but it would have been an elevated status among working class colored and black Jamaicans.

Florizel and Joseph, then, were two outsiders. For Joseph, Moses, and the other Syrian Jews, there was no welcome for them from the Jamaican Jewish establishment. These new arrivants were considered penniless emigrants and viewed as bereft. There was no shared provenance of hundreds of years of settlement, no collective understanding of having made themselves the ultimate powerful minority out of sheer will and hard work and activist politics and applied intellect. They may have been at synagogue each week, but attending the Shabbat services was not essential for Jamaican Jews to maintain their privileged place in the society. Anti-Semitism reinforces one's faith; Jamaican Jews had no such force pushing them to be more observant, more devout.

Joseph, however, who had once studied to be a rabbi, maintained a Jewish household up until his death, and was committed to Jewish causes around the world. Through him, Florizel's name appeared regularly in the newspapers shortly after their marriage, in late 1914 and early 1915. Along with her in-laws, Moses and Abraham, and their wives, she was a regular donor to the cause of persecuted Jews in Poland.

Joseph and Florizel were also among the few Jews in Jamaica who saw to the Gibraltar Camp Jews in Mona, where today the University of the West Indies is headquartered. During World War II, 260 European Jewish refugees, mainly Polish and Dutch, were interned among some two thousand evacuees from Gibraltar and Britain's Mediterranean colonies at what is still called Gibraltar Camp.[23] In general, there was a lack of interest in these Jews among the local Jewish community; most Jamaican Jews treated them "like lepers."[24] Joseph proved one of the few exceptions, likely because Joseph didn't consider himself a part of the Jamaican-Jewish community. Throughout his life, Joseph continued to observe the Jewish holy days by closing his store.

Was it Joseph's vision, to establish a line that would bring the Matalon name, unheard of in Jamaica before his brother Moses's arrival in 1900, to be among the most recognized of Jamaica's most prominent families just half a century later? A name so consonant with power and wealth that it has been repeated in popular songs decade after decade since the 1960s as the epitome of having made it to the top? After being shunned by the establishment Jamaican Jews, considered a nobody, a hawker, could Joseph have conceived that the Matalon name would, in just four decades after his unnoticed arrival, be considered in the same ambit as the elite Jamaican Jews? That his family would, in just a generation, be the most prominent and well-known Jewish family in Jamaica? Could Joseph have imagined that his family would come to epitomize the popular notion of wealthy Jamaican Jews?

Joseph died before the state of Israel was created. But could he have ever thought that one of his sons—Aaron—and later one of his grandsons—Joseph M., Mayer's son—would be a Jewish state's representative in Jamaica, and that his sons would have such influence over the Jamaican government as to influence their votes in an international body to favor a Jewish state? That a diplomat from that Jewish state would do his family the honor of describing his children as a "fortunate mix of the Maccabees and the Rothschilds"?[25]

All this came from the line that Joseph established. His brothers who came to Jamaica did not stay. Abraham apparently went to England in 1926, leaving no further trace.[26] His brother Moses, who was in Jamaica before him, established no roots. He and his English wife, Rose Tawil, had five children born on the island: Isaac, Vivian, Adele, Nisim and Lily, all of whom moved to England in 1955. Vivian, an actor, returned to Jamaica to perform at the Glass Slipper nightclub in the 1950s, and was briefly, in 1970, the honorary director of the Little Theatre Movement, a dramatic arts group in Kingston.[27] Notably, Vivian went on to become an acclaimed director of musicals and plays on the West End and Broadway. Jamaica, apparently, was never intended to be a final destination for any of them. One hundred years after the Levantine Jews came to Jamaica, Joseph's family was the only one that remained on the island. Could Joseph have had any inkling what was to follow from his union with his beautiful flower, Florizel?

Joseph left no records, no diaries, no papers. He was not recorded in the newspapers except for the announcement of his marriage to Florizel, a lawsuit he brought against some of his debtors in 1914, and his donations to the cause of persecuted Jews in Poland. He was a refugee of sorts, transient for much of his adult life, with no homeland to claim, to hark back or return to. He more likely envisioned establishing his own little world with Florizel. With the eleven children they quickly brought forth, he created a self-contained family haven. They would maintain a strict Jewish household that cleaved closely to the faith, and to orthodox Jewish notions of family. They wouldn't need anyone else but each other.

KINGSTON, 3 MARCH 1922

For Joseph and Florizel, 1922 starts with a bounty. They welcome their sixth child, and fourth son, Mayer Michael Matalon (fig 2.1). He joins Pauline, Isaac known as Zackie, Leah, Aaron and Moses. After Mayer came Eleyahu also known as Eli, Gloria, Owen, Adele and, in 1934, the eleventh and last child, Vernon, all born into a Jewish family in a small Jewish minority, free to practice their religion at home and in the outside world. Joseph is strict and conservative, a traditional patriarch, buttressed by his faith and its rituals.

But the year ends badly, a harbinger of things to come. Joseph, seeking to expand his business interests, now in the name of Matalon and Company, purchases large quantities of materials. But the economy takes a downturn, and he loses everything. He can't pay his creditors. Joseph takes the family to Falmouth to start business there. It doesn't work out. He goes back to Kingston. Then Montego Bay. Twice, in quick succession, his business is literally wiped out by floods. He is forced into bankruptcy. His family is destitute.[28]

Around 1935, Joseph moves the family back to a small house in Rae Town in Kingston.[29] He borrows money to pay rent. Joseph, nearly sixty, fueled by the need to feed his large family, goes back to where he started: selling dress lengths on credit door to door. Pauline and Zackie are now young adults, nearly twenty, and they go out to work. Together they pay the rent and put food on the table.

There is no money for school fees. High schooling in the 1930s and 1940s was for the upper classes—for those who had the ability to pay, and a small number of children who showed particular intellectual promise.[30] For the Matalons education is a luxury, but one which they, as all striving families do, recognize as necessary for their future prospects. Aaron, Moses and Mayer have to leave Jamaica College,[31] one of the most prestigious boys' schools in the island for the favored white, near-white and brown sons of the commercial and professional elites. School fees are £5 a term and they don't have it. A Ms. Brenda Smythe and another lady named Adele Murray coach Mayer and Moses to sit for a scholarship at Wolmer's Boys' School and Jamaica College; only ten were awarded each year in Jamaica. Finally,

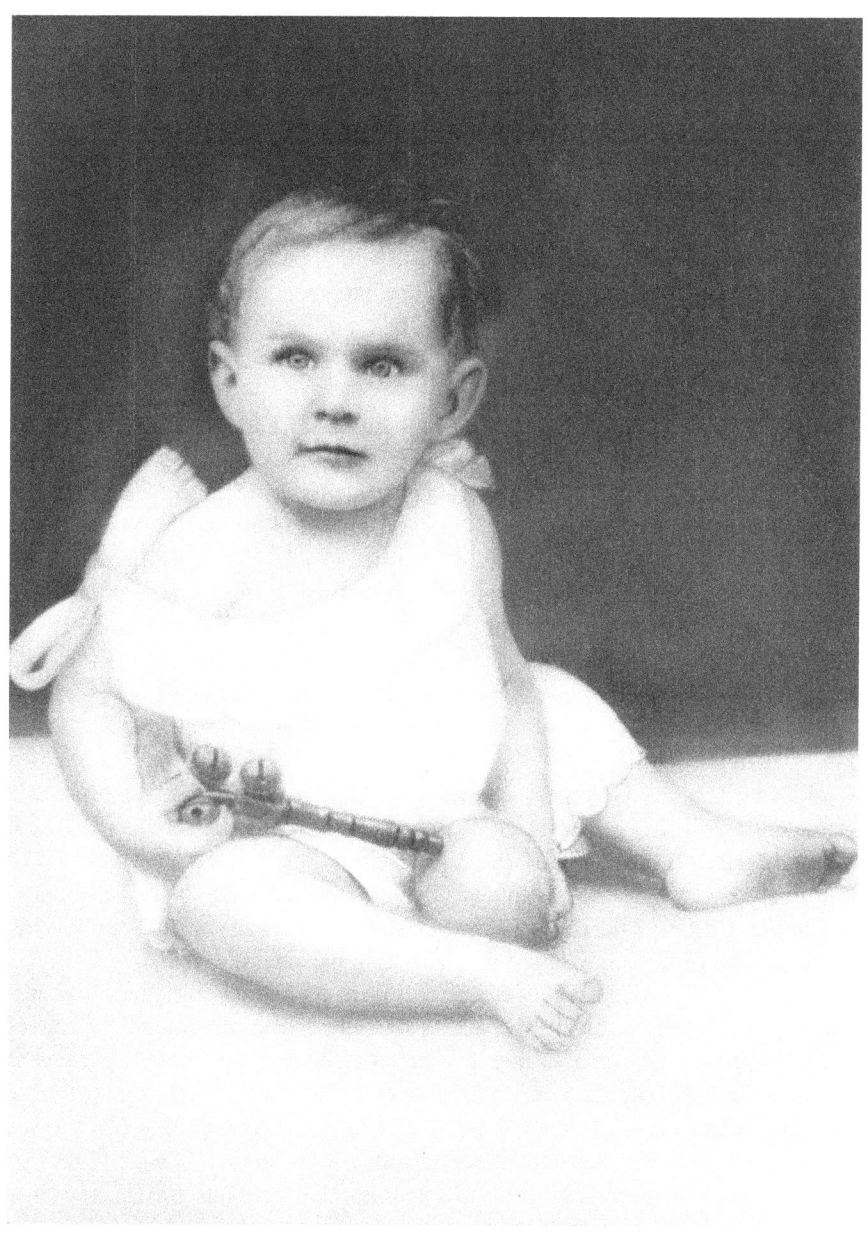

Figure 2.1.   Mayer as a baby, 1922.
Photo courtesy of Joseph M. Matalon.

a breakthrough: Moses and Mayer win two of the scholarships.[32] More relief comes when George Penso, their landlord and friend, puts up the money for Joseph to modestly expand his business.

At Jamaica College, Mayer shows a genius for mathematics. He will become renowned for his ability to calculate numbers in his head. Among his schoolmates is the future prime minister, Michael Manley, son of Norman, one of Jamaica's founding fathers. They become close friends, a friendship which will shape their lives for decades to come.

Jamaica College in the 1930s was distinguished for counting among its alumni many Jamaica and Rhodes Scholars, and many outstanding athletes, whose names and photographs were displayed in the school's main building for all to see and aspire to.

Modeled after the mid-Victorian English public school, scholarship, sport and leadership were the school's priorities. Many of the boys were boarders; Mayer Matalon and his brothers were day students. Most of the teaching staff were British expatriates, as was the norm for other elite secondary schools in Jamaica in the 1930s and right up to the mid- to late-1970s. They inculcated the students, in the classroom and out, with resilience, objectivity, and a sense that each of them was destined for greatness.[33] Mayer's headmaster was R. M. "Reggie" Murray, an Old Boy (former student) who epitomized the ideal JC student: a World War I hero, a Rhodes Scholar, an accomplished marksman and a cricketer. The boys accorded him a status comparable to an ancient Greek hero.[34]

Outside Jamaica College's gates, the political climate was feverish and rising to a boil. Mayer Matalon's time at Jamaica College coincided with the widespread discontent with Jamaica's Crown Colony government, which culminated in what became known as the 1938 Labor Riots. Norman Manley, a Jamaica College Old Boy of great distinction, was at the forefront of the Jamaican nationalist movement toward self-government.

Mayer paid keen attention and, like many of his schoolmates, was imprinted with the patriotism and sense of duty that characterized much of his generation who came of age at that time. One of his contemporaries at Jamaica College, the acclaimed Jamaican poet, M. G. Smith, captured the zeitgeist in the iconic poem, "I Saw My Land in the Morning."[35] Though many Jamaicans may consider this poem an ode to Jamaica's beauty, read in the context of Jamaican politics and social unrest in the late 1930s, it is clear that it is much more a battle hymn:

> *Let the thunder shake*
> *The old Gods awake*
> *Past and future break.*
> *I saw my land in the morning*

And O but she was fair
The hills flamed upward scorning
Death and failure here.

I saw through the mists of morning
A wave like a sea set free
Faith to the dawn returning
Dark tide bright unity.

I saw my friends in the morning
They called from an equal gate
"Build now: whilst time is burning
Forward before it's late."

Then Jamaica
Let the thunder shake
The old Gods awake
Past and future break
On as the voices roll

Move as a single whole
Forward
Forward
Forward
O country to your goal.

These role models, influences and events were critical in shaping Mayer Matalon's sensibility and outlook on the world, and his own place in it.

At home, the Matalon household is brimming with children. Mayer is the sixth child, five more join the family after him; the last, Vernon, is born in 1934 while Mayer is at Jamaica College. Gloria and Adele are enrolled in the United Congregation of Israelites School.[36] Zackie and Pauline have joined the workforce. Aaron, aged thirteen when the family falls on hard times, is too old for a scholarship; he goes out to work as an office boy at Justin McCarthy, a stationers on King Street, and so is able to contribute to the family pot.[37] The only one to leave the family home, Zackie, manages to go to Beirut,[38] where there are relatives on his father's side, to study medicine.

Joseph soon employs Aaron in his own dry goods business, in a similar capacity to his previous job at the stationers, but with a small raise in pay. The story is that there are two pairs of "going out" pants for the boys, and there is a roster determining whose turn it is to wear them. Eli and Mayer, it is said, share a pair of shoes. Pauline, as Florizel later recounts, has three dresses: one on, one off and one in the wash. When Mayer's Red Knight bicycle is stolen he reports it to the police undoubtedly in an effort to get it back because without it he can't get to school, cycling from home at West Avenue in Kingston Gardens all the way up to JC each day.[39] But the family is back on its feet, however modestly.

Mayer leaves Jamaica College in 1938, aged sixteen, after completing the Cambridge School Certificate. There is no option for him to continue to sixth form to do the Higher School Certificate, much less any prospect of university. He wants to study law, a dream and desire that he holds on to for many years. But he must go out to work. He goes on the road selling dry goods for his father.

World War II breaks out in 1939, and some of the brothers join the Allied forces: Zackie in the Eighth Army and Moses in the Royal Navy; Eli, who has lied about his age, enlists in the Royal Canadian Air Force. Aaron stays in the shop with his father. Mayer ventures to Panama where he finds work with the United States Canal Authority for a few years.[40]

Joseph passes in 1944 while on a trip to the United States. He is sixty years old and has had a hard life. Uprooted from a volatile home and essentially in transit for over ten years in a foreign land, he made his home in yet another distant place and culture. Despite dying with the cloud of bankruptcy hanging over his name, he was rich in children, family and faith. With no evidence at the time of his death that his children will in just a few years rise far above their station, he nevertheless has a sense of what is to come for his family, for his name.

His legacy to his children is an admonition to be united: "See this deck of cards? If you take each card individually you can easily tear each one. But if the cards stay together, the deck is solid and impenetrable. If you and your brothers and sisters can stay together, the strength that you may find in that unity will be like a pack of cards. Singly, some of you may be as weak as the individual card."[41]

Where was Mayer in Joseph's vision? Was he to be first among equals? The one Joseph anointed to forge the family's path? There is unlikely to be agreement on this question among those who might know the truth, though what transpires may lend credence to the proposition that Joseph saw Mayer as the favored son. Regardless, Mayer took that role unto himself.

NOTES

1. Carol Holzberg, *Minorities and Power in a Black Society: The Jewish Community of Jamaica* (Lanham, MD: The North-South Publishing Company, 1987).

2. Judith Laikin Elkin, *The Jews of Latin America* (New York: Holmes & Meier, 1998).

3. David Nicholls, "No Hawkers and Pedlars: Arabs of the Antilles," in *Haiti in Caribbean Context: Ethnicity, Economy, and Revolt*, ed. David Nicholls (England: Oxford, 1985), 135–64.

4. Liz Hamui-Halabe, "Re-creating Community: Christians from Lebanon and Jews from Syria in Mexico, 1900–1938," in *Arabs and Jewish Immigrants in Latin America: Images and Realities*, ed. Ignacio Klich and Jeffrey Lesser (London: Frank Cass, 1994), 124–45.

5. Marilyn Delevante and Anthony Alberga, *The Island of One People: An Account of the History of the Jews of Jamaica* (Kingston: Ian Randle Publishers, 2006).

6. Patrick Bryan, *Edward Seaga and the Challenges of Modern Jamaica* (Kingston: University of the West Indies Press, 2009).

7. Nicholls, "No Hawkers."

8. Louise Fawcett and Eduardo Posado-Carbo, "Arabs and Jews in the Development of the Colombian Caribbean 1850–1950," in *Arabs and Jewish Immigrants in Latin America: Images and Realities*, ed. Ignacio Klick and Jeffrey Lesser (London: Frank Cass), 57–79.

9. Elaine Ferguson, "The Growth of an Empire—The Matalon Story," *Money Index* 323, no. 9 (June 1992): 21–50.

10. Brian L. Moore and Michele A. Johnson, *Neither Led nor Driven: Contesting British Imperialism in Jamaica, 1865–1920* (Kingston: University of the West Indies Press, 2004).

11. Nicholls, "No Hawkers."

12. Ibid.

13. Ibid.

14. Ferguson, "The Growth of an Empire."

15. Laikin, *The Jews of Latin America*.

16. Ferguson, "The Growth of an Empire."

17. Holzberg, *Minorities and Power in a Black Society*.

18. Thomas G. August, "An Historical Profile of the Jewish Community of Jamaica," *Jewish Social Studies* 49, nos. 3–4 (Summer–Autumn 1987): 303–16.

19. Rebecca Tortello, *Pieces of the Past: A Stroll Down Jamaica's Memory Lane* (Kingston: Ian Randle Publishers, 2007).

20. As many interviews were conducted in confidentiality, the names of interviewees are withheld by mutual agreement. Personal interview with acquaintance of Mayer Matalon, May 20, 2015.

21. Nicholls, "No Hawkers."

22. "Service of Reconsecration at the Jewish Home," *Gleaner*, March 18, 1946, 3.

23. Joanna Newman, "Refugees from Nazism in the British Caribbean," in *The Jews in the Caribbean*, ed. Jane S. Gerber (Portland, OR: The Littman Library of Jewish Civilization), 343–59.

24. Fred Mann, *A Drastic Turn of Destiny* (Toronto: Second Story Press, 2009).

25. Benno Weiser Varon, *Professions of a Lucky Jew* (New York: Cornwall Books, 1992).

26. In newspaper items from 1915–1926 mention is made of Isaac Matalon. There is no other record or recollection of an Isaac Matalon from that generation. Both Joseph and Moses had the middle name Isaac, so Isaac may be one of them going by their middle name, or simply a journalistic error.

27. "Vivian Matalon to Head Theatre School," *Gleaner*, March 8, 1970, 5.

28. Aaron Matalon, "Growing up in Kingston," Twelfth Annual Bustamante Lecture, Kingston, Jamaica, February 26, 1998.

29. Ferguson, "The Growth of an Empire."

30. Bryan, *Edward Seaga*, 19–20.

31. Ferguson, "The Growth of an Empire."

32. Matalon, "Growing up in Kingston."

33. Charles Levy, *Hash and Roast Beef: A Memoir of Life as a Schoolboy at Jamaica College 1943–1949* (Spokane, WA: Griffin Publishers, 1995).

34. Levy, *Hash and Roast Beef*.

35. M. G. Smith, *In the Kingdom of Light: Collected Poems*, ed. Wayne Brown (Kingston: Mill Press, 2004).

36. The United Congregation of Israelites was formed in Jamaica in 1921, a merger of the Amalgamated Synagogue that was mainly comprised of the Jamaican descendants of Sephardic Jews, and the Ashkenazi Synagogue.

37. Matalon, "Growing up in Kingston."

38. Delevante and Alberga, *Island of One People*, 164.

39. "Arrests Yesterday," *Gleaner*, November 5, 1938.

40. Delevante and Alberga, *Island of One People*, 165.

41. This story was repeated by virtually every Matalon interviewed, and by many other interviewees.

Chapter Three

Early Years in Business

This country is the land of opportunity. Why, it is just opening up. It is going places in a mighty way and we hope to go with it. We are prepared to work harder than anyone else; we are prepared to give our people the kind of service they have never had before, modern, efficient service. We are prepared to invest our profits in service. We know we can't lose. And above all, we intend to stick together as one unit, one team.

Mayer Matalon, 1957[1]

Between 1940 and 1945, Mayer Matalon went to Panama to work in the US Base Authorities' Panama Canal Commission as a base inspector (fig. 3.1).

When he returned to Jamaica he established a tire retreading business in Penso's Garage on Orange Street; motor vehicles and supplies were rationed and retreaded tires were in high demand. Three of his brothers—Zackie, Moses and Eli—had joined various Allied forces and fought in the war. Pauline, the first born and oldest sister, also went to Panama. It was there that Pauline met her husband, an American salesman who had joined the US Army, Jack Goodman. Aaron remained in Jamaica, and ran Matalon and Company on Orange Street in Kingston with his father, selling cloth. The business had grown over the years, though it was still a relatively modest enterprise; Aaron took it over when his father died unexpectedly in 1944.

When the war ended, everyone reunited in Kingston, including Pauline and Jack. Matalon and Company was not big enough to support them all; indeed only Aaron worked there. Moses went to work at Masterton's engineering plant. He later bought a small engineering works on Luke Lane from Masterton. Eli managed the cocoa and confectionery plant at Jamaica Cocoa Products. Mayer wanted to move on from the tire retreading business into something that didn't get his hands so dirty. He wanted to be a lawyer, but at

Figure 3.1. Mayer with his boss in the US Base Authorities Panama Canal Zone, around 1943.
Photo courtesy of Joseph M. Matalon.

that point he couldn't see how that could work, given the need to earn a living for himself, and his calling to be a part of a family effort to create something more than they ever had, for all of them.[2]

The Matalons came to business greenfield, starting from scratch with virtually no capital and little access to credit, but with some experience of working on the road and in the shop with their father. Pauline's experience as a secretary was invaluable, and Mayer brought his own knowledge of inventory management and control from his time in Panama. They pooled together the cash savings they had, borrowed some money, and got an overdraft from the bank for the startup capital to begin trading. What they lacked in capital and experience they made up for in intelligence and willingness to work. Their goal was to find a business that required "a minimum of capital and a maximum of effort."[3]

The initial family venture in 1946, Commodity Service Company Limited at 88 Orange Street in Kingston, was formed by Mayer, Pauline and Jack; it was so generally named because they didn't know exactly what type of business they would engage in at the outset,[4] though the initial idea was that they would be commission agents, the local representatives and distributors for imported goods. Pauline managed the business. Within a few years Aaron brought Matalon and Company into Commodity Service Company as a subsidiary.

They had many advantages. First, as Aaron once put it, they had the "providence of prolific parents."[5] There were many of them, and especially when starting out in a family business, the advantages that a group of siblings brings are invaluable. They can share resources and keep their personal costs down in a way that individuals each coming from different households cannot. And so they did in the early days, sharing houses and cars. On Cunningham Avenue, Mayer lived with Aaron and his wife Marjorie. On nights out at the Glass Bucket nightclub on Half Way Tree Road—the premier entertainment spot for Kingston's elite—the car would make two trips for the brothers and their wives (those who were married) as they were too many to fit at once.

An ideal situation—which by all accounts the Matalons enjoyed at the start—the siblings all came from the same background with common values and ways of understanding the world around them. They trusted each other, both with money and judgment, which has incalculable benefits to a fledgling business.

The Matalon siblings' unity stemmed not only from their joint quest for success—Aaron used to say that they worked while others slept—but in their shared identity as outsiders. Though their father was from Damascus, they had little in common with the other Syrian immigrant families in Jamaica, who were mostly Christian. Nor, as the offspring of a "nobody Jew" and a recently arrived "hawker," were they of the Jamaican Jewish elite. Israel was a newly formed nation, and in any case they had no ties to any family they might have had there, and so couldn't claim the Jewish state for themselves. They were phenotypically white but being Jewish were considered "lesser than" by the Jamaican colonial elite who were mostly British or British descendants.

They were intelligent, including those who had not been able to complete school. They possessed an entrepreneurial instinct, together with prescient foresight into emerging market trends and shifting consumer preferences.

One of their most important early innovations was that they saw that a focus on customer service would bring a good return on investment. Much like their forebears in the textile trade at the turn of the century, they recognized that their business depended on their customers' loyalty and they treated them well. As they participated more in the Jamaican marketplace, importing and distributing, they also saw where there were new opportunities in manufacturing, enabled by more sophisticated machinery and changing consumer preferences, toward more refined and better packaged foodstuffs.

Though they were not of the establishment elite, the boys had gone to school with its sons. They spoke and behaved like their better-off peers. In addition, and importantly, they were white. Their Jewishness compromised their skin color in a context where anti-Semitism and prejudice prevailed among much of the British colonial elite, but those attitudes were on their way to becoming passé. In the context of a social hierarchy where phenotype is a distinguishing factor, their whiteness was an advantage. They also had the underdog's paradoxical advantage: when you have nothing to lose, the sky's the limit.

Commodity Service Company's first commercial activity was wholesale distribution. Distribution agencies were a standard business operation in a colony like Jamaica, which produced virtually nothing for itself. They were essential actors in import dependent economies. As a business, it was also not far removed from their father's own profession. But by the late 1940s markets had gotten more sophisticated, with revolutions in production processes and marketing, and an expansion in the consumer goods market, allowing space for new products and innovations in service delivery. The brothers recognized the openings in a post-World War II Jamaican economy in the context of the changed international economy. Jamaica imported virtually all of its consumer goods and many foodstuffs, but they identified new market openings, and moved quickly to incorporate them as technology, tastes and new goods were developed.

They were not immediately successful, as few startup businesses are. The account given is that at the end of their first year they had a staff of seven and lost £600. Year two they had a staff of fifteen and lost another £1,500. Year three, losses of another £1,000 with a staff of thirty. From there they made a profit; Aaron said in an interview some years later that from then on they "never looked back."[6]

One of their first successes, emblematic of their early adopter's eye for products and markets, was with pharmaceutical distribution. The pharmaceutical industry in the late 1940s was undergoing a transformation. A host of wartime advancements in fermentation and purification technologies had changed the drug development process, and these advances brought massive changes to the way drugs were prescribed, manufactured and distributed. By the end of World War II, a process of consolidation in the US pharmaceutical industry, together with technological, scientific and organizational advances on the part of US drug companies, transformed the industry and the market for drugs.[7] Jamaica, given its geographical location, was a natural market for US drugs, and Jamaican consumers and patients' tastes were rapidly becoming more sophisticated.

Jack Goodman, who had been in drug sales in the United States before meeting Pauline in Panama, was the linchpin in this venture. He was aware of the changes in the industry and recognized the opportunity in Jamaica to be the first in the door. In landing the agency for Burroughs Wellcome Pharmaceuticals, and later Pfizer and Ortho, the Matalons and Goodman broke ground in establishing the first modern drug distributorship and later the first modern pharmacy in Jamaica. (Burroughs was one of the biggest drug manufacturers then; it later merged with Glaxo, of what is today GlaxoSmithKline.) They established Pharmaceutical Services on Laws Street, the first of its kind. Doctors would now send their patients there with prescriptions rather than dispensing medicines from their offices. As the pharmaceutical business grew and deepened, they started a new company, Comserv Pharmacies Ltd., and opened the trailblazing Oxford and York pharmacies, that sold not only drugs, but had a US-style soda fountain where people could sit at a counter and order hamburgers and milkshakes; this was a completely foreign concept in Jamaica, and one which was a hit with the middle and upper classes.[8] These pharmacies sold a wide variety of other items, including fashion. This innovation was but one of the many firsts that the Matalons would bring to different areas of business in Jamaica, and was one of the first examples of their entrepreneurial audacity.

The drug agency was a lucky break, perhaps, given that their awareness of this opportunity came through Pauline's fortuitous choice of husband. But quite typical of the first twenty years of the Matalons' exploits was their use of information to identify opportunities and then vigorously pursue those opportunities.

The Matalons had another important advantage during that time. In tandem with starting Commodity Services Company, the Matalons became involved with the People's National Party (PNP). They would have been one of the only, if not the only, Jamaican Jewish family to support the PNP from the outset. Most Jewish Jamaicans were supporters of Bustamante and the Jamaica Labour Party (JLP).

It was the advent of a new political era in Jamaica. With universal adult suffrage in 1944, the political landscape in Jamaica underwent a seismic change. The granting of the vote to all Jamaicans meant that political parties now had an entirely new constituency to appeal to for votes. Prior to suffrage, politics in Jamaica sought to protect the interests of the landed minority, which in Jamaica meant largely maintaining the status quo's dominant actors' ability to earn profits on their assets and to control the majority black population. With the majority black population now having the power to determine the outcome of the election, political parties sought to appeal to their needs and desires through populist politics and policy.[9]

The PNP were in Opposition after the 1944 elections and, under Norman Manley, were engaged in a rigorous intellectual process of determining what policies would best serve Jamaica and Jamaicans in the future. The Matalon brothers, especially the older ones, were engaged in these discussions. Their support of the PNP and the close ties they forged with its principals from the mid-1940s gave them a front row seat to what government policies were likely to look like in the years to come, as well as a voice in formulating the ideas behind them. They would have inserted their understanding of commerce and advocated for policies conducive to a business-friendly environment at the same time as their participation in those discussions would have given them an in-depth understanding of government policy and its implications for business.

What this meant was not necessarily, as Edwin Allen, opposition JLP member of Parliament for North West Clarendon, later claimed in the House of Representatives in 1957, that the Matalons were given special subsidies, inside information, or preferential concessions.[10] While Allen may have been voicing what many were whispering, he had no proof of his accusations, and his statements amounted to speculation. They were not granted exclusive access, but the Matalons did bring an expertise and understanding of government policy to their entrepreneurial activities, particularly to the prospects for and intricacies of the distribution trade and manufacturing in a context of import substitution policies in a growing consumer economy.[11] Furthermore, the question of preferential treatment has to be cast within the realities of a small island at that stage of development. There were few if any who were in a position financially and attitudinally to pursue the aggressive paths that the Matalons did.

Another aspect of their input, Mayer's in particular, was the recognition and recommendation that sound economic policy should also be shaped to benefit the less well-off as much as possible. This was a pragmatic viewpoint that was buttressed by his own experiences. This led to Mayer being seen as not simply trying to feather his own nest, and further strengthened the confidence that the political leadership then, and in decades to come, would have in seeking out his advice.

From the mid-1950s onward, Commodity Services Company expanded and was soon importing and distributing foods, industrial machinery and equipment, chemicals, fertilizers, oils, lubricants and steel aluminum sheeting. It later added services, namely insurance and shipping, and commission agencies. It distributed locally manufactured goods, such as toilet paper and paper bags, metal beds, biscuits and tomato juice. In the grand scheme these may have been small-scale exploits, but in the context of the tiny economic and consuming elite of Kingston at the time they were brand new pursuits, and were perceived as sophisticated and innovative.

Before the Matalons' major housing and infrastructure projects, two of their other early business successes centered around the importation, packaging and distribution of rice from Guyana, and the packaging and distribution of refined cocoa. After the War, while Mayer, Pauline and Jack went into business together, and Aaron kept Matalon and Company going, Eli had gone into cocoa and confectionery. He managed and then purchased Jamaica Cocoa Products from J. C. Scowan in 1949. As its owner he streamlined the factory and product lines, closing the production of sweets and focusing on a refined cocoa powder for local drinking cocoa under the names Bonnie Breakfast Cocoa and Full Flavour Cocoa Powder, and exporting cocoa butter to make chocolate and cure tobacco. Cocoa manufacturing was a protected industry and there were only two manufacturers in Jamaica at the time; the market for these consumer-friendly products was there for the taking.

One of the agencies Commodity Services Company held was the Caribbean distributorship for Jamaica Knitting Mill. In Mayer Matalon's travels through the region on sales missions for the company he had recognized the opportunity to import rice from Guyana. He negotiated a contract, working between the Jamaica Trade Board for the import license and the Guyana Rice Marketing Board through which all rice exports had to pass. Commodity Services Company became the first distributors of packaged rice in Jamaica, upsetting the market and displacing the traditional suppliers of this basic food item.

Jamaicans were accustomed to purchasing most basic food stuffs by asking the vendor for a certain weight of the item and it being packaged on the spot, usually in brown paper. With rice and cocoa the Matalons introduced prepackaged food items to the market. It was an innovation in the marketing of goods that the Matalons, among others, brought to Jamaica.

The Matalons then ventured into manufacturing. With import substitution policies beginning to be put in place, there was scope for the local manufacture of consumer goods, once the permits and licenses to import the components were secured. With no competition from cheaper imports there was a virtually guaranteed market. Many of the British goods that had been imported began to be produced in Jamaica, and there was scope for local manufacturers to produce for the domestic market.

The idea of import substitution is straightforward: curtail imports of goods that can be manufactured domestically. In theory, the country becomes more self-sufficient, less susceptible to external forces and less dependent on foreign trade. Domestic production is strengthened leading to the creation of domestic industries, value-added activities, job creation and wealth generation, with the possibility of expanding exports.[12] This was the framework employed by many developing countries in the post-World War II period, and many countries enjoyed significant growth (though whether it was as a result of those policies or not is debatable).

In the case of Jamaica, its origins as a colonial plantation economy meant its economy was traditionally dependent on agricultural exports and the importation and distribution of consumer goods. As the political aspiration to structurally transform the economy and empower the masses of poor unskilled Jamaicans took hold, the import substitution idea was attractive.

The Matalons correctly identified the prospects in manufacturing, as the sector grew in tandem with the economy. GDP increased from $296.9 million in 1954 to $902.4 million in 1962, with manufacturing output increasing from $39 million in 1954 to $135 million in 1972. It is important to note, however, that, as a share of the economy, manufacturing hardly grew, from 13 percent in 1954 to only 15 percent in 1972, and imports rose exponentially during those years as the majority of components of domestic manufacturing had to be imported. (In Jamaica during this time, very few manufactured goods were exported.) The Matalons came to be part of an emerging domestic light-manufacturing group primarily comprised of family firms.[13] The Mahfood brothers, who started Caribbean Metal Products (CMP) in 1954, one of Jamaica's first and most preeminent metal furniture manufacturers, would have belonged to this group along with the Matalons.

The policies of post-1950s governments, including import substitution, did not bring about structural change to the Jamaican economy. The two areas of real growth in the 1954–1972 period were mining and tourism, both directly linked to the postwar growth of the US economy. From the 1950s, Jamaica had significant foreign investment in the bauxite/aluminum industry. Tourism also grew as the Jamaican tourism product was refined and made attractive to the US market, and as leisure travel grew among increasingly wealthier North Americans. However, a large proportion of capital investment in these sectors was foreign, and the returns on those investments were usually expatriated.

An economy dependent on external sources of capital is subject to the decisions of those external actors and decision makers. If they deem their capital investment at risk because of a country's instability, investors act accordingly to protect themselves. This came to pass in the 1970s, as foreign investors scaled back on their capital investments and commitments in Jamaica over concerns of instability, and in the case of the bauxite industry, as a direct response to the unilateral imposition of the levy on bauxite ore.

These macroeconomic factors hold important implications for the Matalons' manufacturing interests further down the road. In the 1970s, the Jamaican economy experienced sharp contractions, a fall in consumer demand, and a shortage of foreign exchange, all of which had adverse implications for the manufacturing sector and the retail trade. For the manufacturing businesses in the Matalon (by that time the ICD Group) conglomerate, the 1970s was when the first seeds of financial distress were planted, seeds which blossomed and bore fruit through the 1980s and which precipitated the 1996 attempt to overhaul the businesses and the by-then large debt burden.

At the time though, in the early to mid-1950s, on the cusp of the surge in the Jamaican economy, the medium and long term implications of the macroeconomic effects of the development strategy would likely not have been so obvious and certainly the troubles of the 1970s were impossible to foresee. The Matalons, along with other entrepreneurs, gleaned the business possibilities inherent in the policies of the day and the policies to come, and invested accordingly.

What would have set the Matalons apart, perhaps put them slightly ahead of the pack, would have been their knowledge of the finer points of policies, the bureaucracies that implemented them, and the key people in those bureaucracies. They were able to predict business possibilities not only in the immediate future, but to anticipate demands for goods and services that did not yet exist, but likely would or could, given their knowledge of and involvement in the direction of the government's thinking and the policies they would be pursuing.

The Matalons were not unique in occupying such a space, combining their roles in business with their political insight and the information they gathered from their political ties. Such people exist all over the world and in every era. The combination of recognizing opportunities plus having the access to information, networks and contacts to make good on them, and then possessing the capacity, experience, discipline and managerial talent to implement new developments is usually a winning formula for any successful business undertaking. Nor should we consider it, with a twenty-first century lens, problematic. Many fortunes have been made, and continue to be made today, in Jamaica and all over the world, this way. The state policies of the time were subscribed to by both the JLP and the PNP, and whereas the Matalons and their business interests were openly identified with the PNP, there was a parallel family, the Ashenheims, equally identified with the JLP. Indeed insight into government thinking and access to political leadership was common to all the "big families," according to their political allegiance.

Not every venture or idea was a success, but even the thwarted projects make clear the scope and scale of the Matalons' ambitions, and show how keenly they observed their surroundings and the possibilities that they offered. One of Mayer and Eli's early ideas that didn't come to fruition was Jamaica Airways. With Eli's flying credentials from World War II, he and Mayer, in 1946, conceptualized and began work toward an intra-island and inter-island passenger, freight and mail service, and the establishment of a flying school. This would have been among the first attempts to commercialize the development of air services in Jamaica and quite possibly the

Caribbean. A Miami-Kingston air race was among the ideas that Mayer floated, to advertise the island, as well as to bring the excitement of a flying air show to Jamaica. They went as far as looking at airplanes for purchase.[14] Whether anything happened beyond the announcement in the newspapers is unknown, though the project clearly didn't materialize, but the fact that these young men, with practically nothing to their name, could conceive of and pursue such an audacious project, helps us to understand how out-of-the-box the Matalons thought and dreamed, from the very start.

By the mid-1950s the image was of a bold, rising family: Aaron, Mayer and Moses, as Mayer's son later put it, "the three points of the spearhead,"[15] the triumvirate of the group, with five other Matalon siblings (Leah never worked in the business) and brother-in-law Jack Goodman forming the "stout handle." (Zackie was no longer in the business as he had moved to Morant Bay to work with his wife's family's plantation Stanton Estate, in St. Thomas, and Vernon the youngest was still in school.) The brothers, the sisters and their spouses were all directors, sometimes managing directors, of the different companies. Directors' meetings were essentially family gatherings.

Despite their successes and their growing prominence, they still faced prejudice from the elites, included the Jewish establishment, who considered them "hurry-come-ups." This in no way deterred them. They were blackballed when they applied for membership at the then-exclusive Liguanea Club, and so could not go to its famous New Year's Eve party. Aaron put on his own party, bigger and more decadent.

The Matalons' public statements buttressed and promoted the perception of them as a united force, working together. The full page *Gleaner* ad that the Matalons, represented by Aaron, took out to rebut the allegations of improper ties to the government made by Edwin Allen, stated:

> The history of commerce, industry or agriculture in Jamaica clearly indicates whenever a family in unity bands together its resources, ability and energies, it has never failed to be successful. This is the main reason for our success. Due to Providence and prolific parents, we have joined our resources, know-how and energies.[16]

Mayer, already renowned for his gift with numbers, was the financial brain behind all the family's business undertakings. He did more than the math, more than assess the risk and the return. His skill with numbers, together with his negotiating abilities, meant he was the Matalon who was tasked with, and delivered on, finding the money to back the various ventures, and managing all the financial aspects of the enterprises.

One of Mayer Matalon's greatest legacies is as a negotiator. Some say that a negotiator is born not made, that one cannot learn to be a good negotiator:

that it's in the DNA. Mayer Matalon was one of those. This innate skill was no doubt augmented over time. His experience as a teenager on the road selling for his father introduced him to a wide range of people, honed his interpersonal skills, and gave him the ability to talk to people from all walks of life. His extraordinary emotional intelligence gave him an understanding of people's psychology and motivations, and he used that understanding in the negotiating process. He was more than a good listener—he would step into the shoes of the other person, and see the situation from their perspective. This gave him a good sense of people and it also gave him a remarkable ability to manipulate them. He could persuade people without them realizing it.

Mayer Matalon gave people, even high level officials he had met in the context of a business or government-related negotiation, nicknames; they would initially be caught off guard by this unexpected gesture, but, with few exceptions, would soon reciprocate the spirit in which the nickname was given. He lightened intense moments with humor and wit, restoring an air of ease and collegiality to a difficult moment, even when the two sides were stridently opposed to each other. In the middle of a standoff he would burst out, "Don't piss on my back and tell me that it's raining!" There would be a pause in the room as people mentally scrambled to grasp what he had said; then they would look around at each other, gauging how to respond. Within a few seconds they would realize that they were meant to laugh; the tension would be broken and the negotiation would proceed smoothly thereafter.

Another tactic he was known to employ was to get dramatic, gather up his papers and make as though he was going to storm out of the room. This would throw people off guard as this was unexpected and unusual behavior in a high-level negotiation. When it worked, which it usually did, the other party would be distracted from the matter at hand and destabilized by his unpredictability, reactions which he would use to his side's advantage.

He innately knew how to "hide his hand," and work his way to a better outcome. He had an excellent memory, and total recall of anything he ever read or wrote, and so was able to call up facts and past events to bolster his positions and chip away at those of his opponents. His skill at quickly doing complex calculations in his head gave him an advantage in that he always had a ready response to any proposal regarding numbers. His ability to monetize actions and transactions, and to attach costs and numbers to items that previously had no figure attached, allowed him to understand immediately the financial implications of whatever was being negotiated, an angle that he would use to counter the opposing side's proposals. Ced Ritchie, chairman and CEO of the Bank of Nova Scotia (Canada) from 1974–1995, once said of Mayer, that if he (Mayer) had gone up to the Mount instead of Moses he was sure he would have negotiated the Commandments down from ten to only two or three.

At the same time as he ventured forth in business, Mayer also took on the role of opinion leader and influencer, a precursor to his later role as advisor to prime ministers and ministers of finance. From very early on, Mayer's views were sought on a wide variety of public policy issues; he was often cited in the news for his perspective on the issues of the day, particularly those concerning trade and business. While traveling on business throughout the region in the early days of Commodity Services Company, even though he was a young man just in his midtwenties then, he connected with Jamaicans in the other territories that he visited, and on return from his various trips, his views and opinions on politics and business in the colonies became newsworthy items.

The late 1940s was also a stage of consolidation in Mayer's personal life. Known in Kingston social circles for being a dashing playboy, at twenty-six he met and fell in love with Sara Castel, known fondly as Sarita (the Spanish diminutive). Sarita had the distinctive background of having being born in Panama but having spent most of her childhood in the United Kingdom. Her grandfather had been a rabbi in Hebron, a Jewish settlement in what was then Palestine. (In 2019 it is a Palestinian city in the West Bank, south of Jerusalem, with a significant population of Israeli settlers.) He was killed in the unrest from which Mayer Matalon's own father Joseph had fled at the turn of the century. Sarita's ancestors subsequently left their homeland, as Joseph and his siblings had done, and went to Panama where a large number of Levantine Jews had settled, as they had throughout Central America. Panama also had, like Jamaica, a significant population of Sephardic Jews, originating in Spain and Portugal, who had been there for centuries.

Sarita, fluent in English and university educated, was a divorcee; her first husband Nelson Fidanque was from a prominent Panamanian Jewish family, and they had a daughter, Diana. Sarita was four years older than Mayer, a fact that she kept a secret for most of her life. Her own children did not know her age until she was seventy, had suffered a heart attack and was incapacitated; they made the discovery by getting hold of her passport.

Mayer had spent some years in Panama, but he met Sarita in Jamaica. She was visiting her sister Estelle who was married to Felix Shalom, a Jamaican Jew, son of one of the few other Jews who had come to Jamaica in the 1910s and 1920s. Sarita had found a job in New York and had brought her young daughter to Jamaica to stay with Estelle while she settled there. While in Jamaica she met Mayer, who wooed her back from New York. They married on March 31, 1949, in a small ceremony at a house on Hopefield Avenue in Kingston (fig. 3.2). The ring he gave Sarita was his mother's wedding band,

Figure 3.2. Mayer and Sarita's wedding party, March 31, 1949 wedding. L-R, Pauline Goodman (sister), Abraham Shalom (Felix Shalom's father), Florizel Matalon (mother), Estelle Shalom (Sarita's sister), Mayer, Sarita, Eli (brother), Rebeca Castell (Sarita's mother), Aaron (Mayer's brother), Felix Shalom (Sarita's brother-in-law).
Photo courtesy of Joseph M. Matalon.

as he didn't have the money to buy one. The *Gleaner* carried a photo of them and reported that they would honeymoon in Trinidad.

Florizel, Mayer's mother, was against the marriage, not wanting Mayer to marry an older woman and a divorcee. Sarita and Florizel never enjoyed a warm relationship, but Sarita was not remarkable in this regard. Florizel was very protective and possessive of her sons, and didn't take easily to most of her daughters-in-law. When they returned from their honeymoon they lived with Estelle and Felix until they could afford a place of their own.

Just as Joseph had made Florizel truly Jewish, so did Sarita Mayer. She was observant, and kept a kosher household, hewing much more closely to Jewish customs than Mayer's siblings did in their own families, including those who married Jamaican or American Jews, as most of them did. Mayer supported Israel and its existence as a homeland for the Jewish people, but it wasn't a cause to which he devoted much thought or time. Aaron was Honorary Consul for Israel in the 1960s, and often spoke out in favor of Israel and against Jamaican government policy when it seemed to be anti-Israel. Mayer, Sarita and the children once visited Israel on a family trip, around 1968, but their relationship to and identification with Israel was more notional than lived.

The Matalons celebrated the Jewish holidays, usually with large family gatherings and meals at Florizel's, but Zackie was the only one of the siblings who regularly attended synagogue, traveling from Morant Bay. Beyond that there were few if any ties to Israel on the part of the Jamaican Matalons. It is thought that Joseph the father had relatives, maybe even siblings or half-siblings, who had settled in Israel after leaving Damascus, but little effort was ever made to locate them and no connection was made or maintained with them. There are several prominent Israeli Matalons, including an acclaimed novelist, a former member of the Knesset, and a beauty queen who came to international attention for having taken a selfie (photograph) with a fellow Miss Universe contestant from Lebanon. Mayer, while a director of the United Congregation of Israelites (the governing body of Jamaica's Jews) for many years, was himself not very religious; but he went along with Sarita because of his devotion to her. Mayer's repertoire of aphorisms and witticisms for which he was well known included one: "A Jew is like a prostitute; he wants to have it, sell it, and still have it,"[17] which invoked his own religious and ethnic group in unflattering terms. This was his risqué sense of humor on display, rather than any serious aspersion.

Indeed Sarita renewed and deepened the Jewishness of the entire Matalon clan. She remained devout throughout her life; Mayer supported her religiosity, and her raising their children in the faith. Four of them married Panamanian Jews, and Diana, Sarita's first daughter married an Iraqi Jew (see fig. 3.3). All the daughters were committed to, and carried on, the Jewish faith and traditions in their own families.

Sarita brought a worldliness, an elegance, to their marriage, and to Mayer himself. While he could never have been considered in any way rough around the edges, many of Mayer's family members saw him become more refined, more discerning in his tastes, and attributed that to Sarita's influence. He himself said, "I know how to make money, but Sarita gives me class."[18] Nevertheless, Mayer was never diffident about his beginnings. At a London gentleman's club in the 1950s as the guest of Sir Brian Mountain, one of its members, on making his acquaintance, gestured to his tie and asked, "Eton 1940?" "No," he replied irreverently, "Saks Fifth Avenue, last year."[19]

Sarita was an expert bridge player and soon after their marriage she was well established on the local bridge scene, playing in and hosting tournaments on the island. They often appeared in the social pages, having attended New Year's Eve parties at the Myrtle Bank Hotel, or cocktails for a visiting Israeli dignitary at brother Aaron's house, as he was Jamaica's first Honorary

Figure 3.3. Sarita and Mayer on the occasion of their daughter Diana's wedding, London, 1966.
Photo courtesy of Joseph M. Matalon.

Consul for Israel, or themselves hosting a function in Mayer's own capacity as Honorary Consul for Sweden. Their social life was largely Sarita's doing; Mayer would have preferred to stay at home. He was known as a loner, and somewhat antisocial, even when he was a young bachelor.

Over the next ten years, Mayer and Sarita had four more children: Jacqueline, Gail, Rebeca, and at last a son, Joseph, who came to be known as "Joe M.," or "little Joe." (Aaron had also named his son, born some years earlier, Joseph; he became known as "Big Joe" or "Joe A.")

At home Mayer was loving, but strict. His children were required to dress for dinner, including shoes and socks. Even when his daughters thought he was too busy to notice, and they would get ready to leave home in a trendy or fashionable outfit, he would send them back to their rooms to change into more conservative clothing, seeing them with, in their minds, eyes in the back of his head. When he wasn't working he was at the Caymanas racetrack, or preparing for the Saturday races with his horse-loving brothers and friends.

Mayer traveled often during this time, seeking and managing agencies and distribution arrangements throughout the Caribbean, even as far as Suriname. Sarita sometimes traveled with him, adding a vacation to the business trip. They visited Canada, the United States and England on holidays. They purchased a home in London in the 1950s where they stayed on their visits, and where Mayer often spent months at a time, combining business, vacation and his favorite pastime of all, betting on horses.

When he was at home he gardened, tending rose bushes in the various homes he occupied between the 1950s and 1970s. Over a twenty-year period he moved his family to various houses in Kingston, to Sarita's dismay. She wanted to stay in one house but Mayer kept uprooting them, and she would only learn about it after the plans were already too far along to be changed. After moving out of the Shalom's on Chester Avenue they went to a house on Ruthven Road. As the family grew they next lived on Dewsbury Avenue in Barbican. From there they moved to Seymour Avenue, where the Canadian High Commissioner's residence was later established. They moved from there after a fire in one of the girls' bedrooms. Then they moved to the great house at Hughenden, a large property that the family called "the farm." When Hughenden was developed in 1967 by WIHCON into a mass housing estate, the great house was preserved as a community center, which is still in operation. From there they lived briefly in a rented house on Barbican Road, then in a house owned by Eagle Star in Norbrook, which later became Prime Minister P. J. Patterson's home, Uhuru.

At Long Lane, the home Mayer lived in from 1970 until he died, he grew orchids and citrus trees, including the uncommon shaddock fruit that he proudly presented to friends and family. He loved to walk out in the mornings to look at his trees, and, as his children recall, "to cuss whoever was to be cussed" for not looking after them properly.[20] He entered his large purebred dogs in shows, and they won in their categories.[21] He played tennis, and hated to lose. He read widely, and was fond of quoting Shakespeare and poetry. He smoked throughout his life, even when he was much older; when he was in his eighties and ill in the private Tony Thwaites Wing at the University Hospital of the West Indies having had a heart attack, he regularly stepped outside to smoke his cigarettes.

Though not as prodigious an art collector as his brother Aaron, whose collection of paintings and sculptures was one of the largest and most valuable private collections in Jamaica during his time, Mayer Matalon had very specific—and, as it would turn out, lucrative—taste in art. Over the decades that he had his flat in London, the 1950s to the 1990s, he collected the work of the English landscapist L. S. Lowry, and owned a total of six paintings. Lowry's work largely depicted British industrial cities and scenes. When Mayer sold his London flat in the mid-2000s, after Sarita's dementia brought their London sojourns to an end, the collection was auctioned by Christie's, one of the world's most prestigious art auctioneers. The leading piece in the collection, which Mayer had bought at auction in 1970 for £16,800 sold for £3,772,000. Five of the six works put forward sold for a total of £5,972,000.

As the business and staff complement of Commodity Services Company and its associated businesses grew, the Matalons relocated from their Orange Street premises to upstairs the Esquire Restaurant on Barry Street, and from there to the corner of Harbour Street and Fleet Street, where what remains of the original family business is still housed over sixty years later.

The Matalon brothers—though most of the sisters worked in the business they were generally not included in considerations of the family as an entrepreneurial unit—became known not only for their business and professional activities, but for their wit and humor. They ate together every day in the lunch room at Harbour Street up until the mid-1970s. They regularly invited politicians, their friends and their business associates to join them there; some friends didn't need an invitation. Whosoever accepted the invitation—regardless of their "importance"—did so on the understanding that they would be picked apart. That lunch room developed a reputation as being a place of great comedy, but to which one should only venture if one could take intense teasing.

Mayer was the main teaser; he was relentless in making fun of people, though always in a spirit of warmth and affection. He had a nickname for all his brothers, and would assign nicknames to almost everyone else he regularly associated with. Zackie was Farmer, Aaron was Tiger, Moses the Ancient Mariner. Some of the nicknames had obvious connotations, some less so. Eli was the Sheriff, which he later fulfilled, in a way, when he became minister of national security. Owen was Roots or Roots Man, and Vernon was Twinkle Toes; the origins of their names will probably forever be contained in the Harbour Street lunchroom. Other family members, even the very young ones, weren't spared. One very fair skinned niece got the nickname "Casper" after the popular comic book series, Casper the Friendly Ghost. When he later had his own grandchildren, if they had the famous Matalon stick-out ears, they were never allowed to forget it. One thinner-than-the-others grandchild, Gail's daughter Daniella, was "Olive Oyl." A close friend's wife, who had wider-than-average hips, he called "Bantu Batty." Some nicknames, coming from anyone else, would have been considered indecent, offensive even. A businessman whose integrity he had little regard for was an "Anglicized mongoose," and about another man who he really disliked he remarked, "that man would screw a snake if he could just get someone to hold it still!"[22] Mayer's irreverence, coming as it did at a time before twenty-first-century notions of political correctness, was taken in the spirit in which it was delivered: one of drollery and congeniality. This was his unique way of building relationships with people, and if you got a nickname that meant he liked you.

Mayer and Aaron, especially, were known for their obsession with education, probably stemming from their own unfulfilled dreams of pursuing further studies. Aaron, who had to leave school at just thirteen, and Mayer who had wanted to do Higher Schools (a course of study and examinations) and study law, generously organized and funded scholarships and bursaries for others to pursue and complete further education, often concealing that they were the benefactors.

As time went on, the Matalon siblings took up business opportunities as they presented themselves. Roles and tasks were allocated to the sibling they were best suited for, and to those who had the greatest interest, as was the norm for a growing family business. The profits, as they came in, were distributed ostensibly equitably, but without any sort of salary scale that would characterize a non-family venture. This system, or lack of a system, worked for the first three decades, governed by a Marxist ethos, not unusual for families in business together:

> It was easy for us to stay together, because we had come from a closely knit family, so in our business dealings as we did in our family, the older took care of the younger, the weaker was taken care of by the stronger. Each contributed according to their ability and each were satisfied according to their needs. We never divided profits for many, many, many years.[23]

But such an approach, even with the best of intentions, is seldom sustainable as people's interests develop and diverge, as siblings have their own growing families, and as some siblings' families grow larger than others.

But we are far from that point in Mayer Matalon's story.

At the outset in 1946, Mayer Matalon and his siblings had what was seemingly an ideal set up: a band of smart brothers and sisters, outsiders with all the attributes to fit into the mover and shaker set, hungry and with nothing to lose, working together to create something big, in a context where the potential was limitless and the odds were in their favor.

NOTES

1. "Jamaica," *Newday* 1, no. 2 (September, 1957).
2. Ainsley Henriques, "Mayer Michael Matalon: A Reflection and a Tribute," ICD Group website, 2012, www.icdgroup.net. Much of the information about the Matalons' early years was obtained from this eulogy, or from a series of personal interviews with Mr. Henriques from 2015–2018.
3. Martin Mordecai, "Aaron Matalon (interview)," *Jamaica Journal* 19, no. 4 (1986): 11–18.
4. Aaron Matalon, "Growing Up in Kingston."
5. Ibid.
6. Mordecai, "Aaron Matalon."
7. Peter Younkin, "An American Oligopoly: How the American Pharmaceutical Industry Transformed Itself during the 1940s," paper presented at the Annual Meeting of the American Sociological Association, New York, August 11, 2007, www.citation.allacademic.com/meta/p_mla_apa_research_citation/1/8/4/4/1/pages184412/p184412-1.php.
8. Delevante and Alberga, *Island of One People*, 166.
9. Damien King, "On the Origins of the Political Economy of Underdevelopment in Jamaica," unpublished paper, 2013.
10. "Jamaica," *Newday* 1, no. 2 (September, 1957).
11. John Gafar, "An Analysis of Import Substitution in a Developing Economy: The Case of Jamaica," *Caribbean Studies* 18, nos. 3–4 (October 1978–January 1979): 139–56.
12. Ibid.
13. Obika Gray, *Radicalism and Social Change in Jamaica, 1960–1972* (Knoxville: University of Tennessee Press, 1991), 39.
14. "Miami-Kingston Air Race Suggested for Advertising Island," *Gleaner*, March 4, 1946, 3.
15. "Jamaica," *Newday* 1, no. 2 (September, 1957).
16. Ibid.
17. As many interviews were conducted in confidentiality, the names of interviewees are withheld by mutual agreement. Interview with acquaintance of Mayer Matalon, June 15, 2015.
18. Interview with acquaintance of Mayer Matalon, June 14, 2015.

19. Interview with family member of Mayer Matalon, June 2015.
20. Ibid.
21. "Seventh All-Island Dog Show Comes Off Successfully," *Gleaner*, July 8, 1949.
22. Derek Jones, "My Memories of Mayer," personal email to Joseph M. Matalon, March 2012.
23. Matalon, "Growing up in Kingston."

Chapter Four

The Numbers Man

Mayer Matalon is well known for many things: his negotiating skills, his wit and dry humor, his powerful connections and his ability to cultivate relationships with people everywhere he went, his intransigence in holding to his position and low tolerance for anyone who disagreed with him, and his use of salty language without compunction, even in the most formal of settings. Most of all, however, he is known for his proficiency with numbers. His ability to quickly and accurately calculate numbers in his head is legendary. He abhorred the use of calculators and would not allow the people who worked for him to use them; he thought it was a sign of laziness not to be willing to use one's mind.[1] His genius went beyond being good at calculations; he was able to conceptualize financial mechanisms that brought ideas to reality. Among those who were closely associated with him and his businesses, including his public sector work, many considered his greatest attribute to be his ability to size up any situation and identify a financial solution to it.

His aptitude for mathematics, which was recognized when he was a schoolboy at Jamaica College, was key to his receiving the scholarship that enabled him to complete high school. So impressive was it that when his mathematics teacher became the school principal in the 1960s, he appointed Mayer Matalon chairman of the school board, a position he held from 1967–1971.

He brought his adeptness with numbers to one of his favorite pastimes, to which he devoted the most time outside of work: horse racing and the track (fig 4.1). He was a gambler, but not of the throw-the-dice variety; he made his bets based on his own complicated calculations of a wide range of variables. He seldom lost. Lucien Chen, one of the most popular and important bookmakers at Caymanas in the 1960s, stopped taking Mayer's bets because he couldn't make any money off him.

Mayer's daughter Jacqueline joined the family business as a young married woman in 1969, helping her aunt Gloria manage the brothers' personal finances. When her father's check books became her responsibility, she found he kept a separate account for his horse racing bets and wins. She scolded him for gambling, to which he replied, "You take out my winnings and debts from the horse racing and you will see that I am ahead."[2] He always was.

Mayer Matalon took horse racing and betting on horses very seriously, relishing the calculations based on ratings and handicaps. With his horse racing friends, Jack Ashenheim and Dennis Lee, at the advent of computing technology in the late 1960s, Mayer created a handicap form with his own variables on ICD's mainframe computer. On a Friday afternoon the ICD com-

Figure 4.1. Mayer Matalon (right), leading his horse back to the stables at Caymanas Park on March 13, 1967.
Courtesy of the Gleaner Company (Media) Limited.

puter bureau was shut down for regular business and dedicated to running the numbers for the next day's races.

Dell Weller was responsible for collecting the information from the clockers for Mayer to use in making his own ratings (the estimates or predictions of an aspect of a horse's performance in a race). The first call on the Friday was to Weller to get the ratings.

Later on Friday afternoon, brother Vernon, Pat Rousseau and Mayer would go out to the track to inspect each of his horses and talk to the trainers about their prospects for the next day. Mayer would also inspect the other horses, talking to their trainers if he could, as he assessed the competition. He had a deep knowledge of horses, their pedigree, physiology, temperament, breeding and training. Friday night was devoted to discussion and analysis, and making a betting plan for Saturday. On Saturday he was at the races. Mayer, Weller, Pat, and Keith Tang put up their own clocker at Caymanas because they didn't trust the times recorded by the official clockers. Even though they had done the analysis and calculations together, he almost always did better than the other members of his group seated in his box at Caymanas Park.

Horses both consumed and relaxed him. He also bet on horses in England, where again he established his own data source so he could assess the horses and their chances. Through his relationship with Sir Brian Mountain, chairman of British Race Courses, he was invited to attend the races there and cultivated a relationship with an English bookie whom he trusted to place his bets as instructed.

For decades, he was prominent in the Jamaican horse racing community, as an owner and an active member of the Jamaica Racehorse Owners' Association, often negotiating on the Association's behalf with the Caymanas Track Limited in their disputes. He had his own stud farm and stables, Turnbull Farm in St. Catherine, where, with the renowned trainer Paul Newman, he bred horses from the late 1960s to the early 1980s; at one point they had over twenty-five horses on the track.

Turnbull Farm later became a point of controversy when the government bought it from him in 1987 for the construction of low-cost housing in the second phase of the Eltham housing scheme. The company that would do the construction? One of the Matalons' private companies, WIHCON. This was only one of a string of controversies between Mayer, the Matalons' Industrial Commercial Developments (ICD), and the Jamaican government over land transactions. Another instance arose when the government, through the Urban Development Corporation (UDC),[3] bought the Forum Hotel in Portmore in 1982. Originally called the Adventure Inn, the Forum Hotel was an ambitious venture on the part of the Hellshire Development Scheme mounted by another Matalon family entity, the Foreshore Development Company. The hotel operated for one year, 1974–1975, before being closed as unprofitable. The original stated purpose of the UDC's purchase of the hotel was to rehouse elderly residents of the Eventide Home who had been displaced by a fire, though by the time the purchase was finalized that plan had already been scrapped, and there was no designated reason for the building to be bought.[4] The price paid by the government was "far more than the figure recommended by professional evaluators."[5] At the time there was speculation that then-Prime Minister Edward Seaga was doing the Matalons a favor by taking the hotel off their hands, and in doing so injecting much-needed cash into the business, which by then was beginning to be an ailing concern.

A land transaction that garnered even more publicity and was widely discussed for months, if not years, occurred in 1988 when Mayer was chairman of what was then Telecommunications of Jamaica (TOJ), the majority-government owned telephone and communications monopoly. TOJ—with Mayer as chairman—purchased two lots of land from ICD—where Mayer was chairman and shareholder. The transaction led to intense speculation, which played out extensively in the media, that the government paid far more money than the land was worth, despite a valuation by an independent land valuator.[6] When a lawsuit was brought by minority shareholders of TOJ, however, the judge opined that there was not an "iota" of evidence of any corruption or self-dealing.[7] No such controversy ever ruffled Mayer. He was always confident that his dealings could stand up to scrutiny. He declared at the time of the TOJ-ICD deal, "I am not embarrassed because everything I did was above board."

After Paul Newman died in 1985, in the absence of a trusted manager, Mayer's passion for horse breeding waned. He continued to own and co-own racehorses with Pat Rousseau, and his love of horse racing endured. Even after he had sold all his horses and no longer frequented Caymanas, he continued to bet on English horse races, through his longtime bookie in London, until a few years before he died. The track gave him a means to combine his genius for numbers, his penchant for making money, and his love of horses: a winning combination.

NOTES

1. Rousseau, "Tribute."
2. Jacqueline Matalon Malca, personal interview, May 12, 2015.
3. The UDC is a public sector organization responsible for urban development, urban renewal, and rural modernization. Since its inception in 1968 it has come to be a powerful entity due to its control of public lands and resources, and its chairman and board of directors are usually carefully selected from among party loyalists.

4. Colin Blair, "What's to Become of Forum Hotel?" *Gleaner*, September 8, 1990, 2.

5. "Govt. Buys Forum For Price Above Evaluators' Recommendation," *Gleaner*, October 30, 1982, 1.

6. "TOJ Buys Land From ICD Group," *Gleaner*, November 26, 1988, 1.

7. Ferguson, "The Matalons," 19.

Chapter Five

The Growth of ICD

As the Jamaican economy grew and developed, so did the Matalon family's businesses. Mayer Matalon and his brothers often said that what was good for their businesses was good for Jamaica and vice versa—not necessarily an extraordinary view among Jamaican-owned companies in the nationalist era of the 1950s, but also a pragmatic one: Mayer wanted Jamaica to flourish and survive for the sake of the country and his businesses. Up to 1956, the expansion of the latter was primarily comprised of acquiring new agencies for the distribution of imported goods, and the pharmaceutical and drugstore businesses. A critical juncture came with the family's venture into mass housing in 1956 and the creation of West Indies Home Contractors (WIHCON), a development that will be dealt with in a separate chapter. This initiative was important in and of itself, but it also had implications for ICD and its core businesses, which grew proportionate to WIHCON's construction needs.

In 1962, Industrial Commercial Developments (ICD) was formed to house what was becoming a conglomerate—a number of different companies operating different kinds of business. The businesses grew and new ones were created or acquired. The general consensus among their peers in the Jamaican business community was that the Matalons "demonstrated outstanding management capability and entrepreneurial expertise."[1] Though there was no stock exchange in Jamaica then, other investors, besides the family members who were part of Commodity Services Company, began to come on board.

The original company, Commodity Services Company, was, by the early 1950s, profitable enough to support the siblings and their growing families in solid Jamaican privilege. From sharing a pair of long pants and a car, the brothers now each had their own well appointed homes in appropriate neighborhoods, and traveled to the United Kingdom, the United States and Canada, as well as throughout the Caribbean on holidays. Many of the children were sent overseas to boarding schools.

By 1966, when the establishment of the stock exchange in Jamaica provided a platform for ordinary shares in the company to be offered for public subscription, ICD listed five subsidiaries in its share offering: PA Benjamin Manufacturing Company Limited (perfumes, food flavors and coloring, and other household oils and liquids); Tropicair Jalousies (aluminium and PVC windows, doors and roofing material); West Indies Paints; Cecil B. Facey (then the largest food, pharmaceutical and hardware distributor in the island); and Jamaica Cocoa Products. The family made sure of having a controlling interest by retaining just over 50 percent of the shareholdings. Other companies and businesses that were not subsumed in ICD included the substantial share interest acquired in United Motors, importer of General Motors vehicles in Jamaica, in 1960. These were referred to as the "Matalon Group of Companies," a separate, family-owned private entity. To the general public, however, the distinction between which Matalon businesses were privately owned and which were public was lost. The perception was of a large, successful, multi-faceted conglomerate, all owned and controlled by the Matalon family.

By the end of 1969, ICD had acquired interest in or started ten more new businesses in Jamaica. On acquiring Cecil B. Facey, the family merged it with their own agency and distribution businesses in food and hardware, creating Facey Commodity. In 1967 the company acquired Conditionedair and Associated Contractors (CAC), a commercial air conditioning business. It expanded into retail with Brooks Enterprises supermarkets and garment stores, and a new manufacturing business with Caribbean Brush Limited, and then ventured into the very new area of computers with Computer Services Limited. The Matalons started home appliance retail with Homelectrix and the accompanying Home Appliances Finance Corporation, one of the early purveyors of hire purchase in Jamaica, the means by which many working class Jamaicans are able to acquire furniture and appliances. They also ventured outside of Jamaica, purchasing 47.5 percent ownership of ANSA Industries, a refrigerator and cooker manufacturing plant in Trinidad. Between 1966–1969 earnings per ICD share went from 1.3 cents to thirteen.

In the early 1970s expansion continued apace. The Matalons acquired interests in garment manufacturing, Redimix Concrete, International Insurance Brokers, and galvanized sheeting manufacturing, and attempted to diversify into exports with their line of perfume and toilet water manufactured by Benjamin's. By 1977, the ICD Group of Companies had twenty-eight subsidiaries. Foreign investors in ICD included the Commonwealth Development Corporation and Japan's Mitsubishi.

It was at this point that the Matalons were named to the list of the "twenty-one families," compiled by a young UWI lecturer, Stanley Reid. Published in a 1977 book, *Essays on Power and Change in Jamaica*, edited by Carl Stone, who was, at the time, Jamaica's most prominent social and political commentator and pollster, Reid identified these families as the major centers of power in the 1970s. Seven were Jewish, of whom four—Ashenheim, Henriques, DaCosta, and Matalon—were singled out as being particularly influential and, presumably, wealthy.[2] Whether or not Reid's measures of power were relevant, the article was widely discussed, became required reading for UWI students at the graduate and undergraduate levels, cited in UWI academics' scholarly work, and permeated Jamaicans' social consciousness in the midst of an increasingly polarized and racialized polity.

As they continued to add and grow businesses, their employee complement grew in tandem. Over four years, between 1966–1970, the number of employees across all the businesses increased from 411 to two thousand. Management challenges often accompany such rapid growth, and the need for in-house training, particularly in management, prompted the purchase of staff training programs from the American Management Association. After losing middle and senior managers to migration in the 1970s, in-house training became an even greater imperative. Within a few years, led by Aaron

Figure 5.1. Mayer with his mother and siblings at her birthday celebration, 1970. L-R back row, Owen, Mayer, Vernon, Eli, Aaron, Zackie, Moses L-R front row, Gloria, Florizel, Pauline, Adele.
Photo courtesy of Joseph M. Matalon.

Matalon, the Institute of Management and Production (IMP) was launched in 1976, and within two years was offering management training to people beyond ICD's own employees.[3] This was the first educational institution of its kind in Jamaica, and predated the University of the West Indies' own Department of Management Studies.

The 1970s were challenging for businesses throughout Jamaica. Like many other businesses, ICD and its subsidiaries were affected by a downturn in sales and productivity, and by the shortage of foreign exchange, which affected imports of raw materials for manufacturing as well as goods for distribution. A wide range of imported consumer goods was banned in the effort to curtail foreign exchange expenditure and to encourage local production.

The economic volatility also brought opportunities for expansion, however. Many companies had failed to adapt to the new economic landscape of 1970s Jamaica, and closed or were sold. The acquisition of Bryden and Evelyn, which, up until the mid-1970s was one of Jamaica's most prominent food and hardware distributors, was one such opportunity for the Matalons. The incorporation of its business into Facey Commodity expanded its product lines and agencies. Through the acquisition of Bryden and Evelyn and, earlier, Cecil B. Facey, the existing and longstanding licenses that they had, allowed the Matalons, and the other companies that had or got licenses, to stay in business when their competitors simply didn't have goods to sell.

As they had from the start, the siblings engaged themselves in different aspects of the business. As they themselves stated in a 1977 journal article of the Jamaica Chamber of Commerce, Jamaica's oldest private business organization: "Aaron's special skill is administration with a special leaning to Marketing; Mayer—Finance and Negotiations; Owen—Operations; Moses—Development and Engineering, responsible for Owen's training; Vernon—sales; Pauline and Adele—pharmacies and pharmaceuticals; Gloria—Commodity Services Company."[4] Eli had run the cocoa factory, and then Tropicair Jalousies and West Indies Paints, but had left the business when he contested a PNP seat for the Kingston Parish Council in 1969. He was elected Councillor and then Mayor of Kingston from 1971–1973. After coming to office in 1972, Michael Manley appointed him minister of state in the Ministry of Education, then minister (of education), and finally minister of security and justice. (Leah, the third child and second daughter of Joseph and Florizel, died in 1971 at the age of fifty-two; she had not worked in the business.)

Regardless of what his official title might have been—director, chairman, president, deputy chairman—Mayer was *de facto* chief financial officer and negotiator for all the businesses. Sourcing the financing for new businesses, expansions and acquisitions, and negotiating the terms, largely fell to him.

The businesses continued to grow and expand despite the difficulties of the 1970s, through the 1980s and into the early 1990s, to the point where they were regarded by the public as an empire. Between ICD and its subsidiaries, WIHCON, and the privately held companies, the Matalons employed thousands of people, educated thousands of people, built thousands of people's houses, and served tens if not hundreds of thousands of customers in their supermarkets and through their products. They may not have been the largest private sector entity in Jamaica in the 1970s and 1980s, but they were certainly perceived as such by many Jamaicans.

Well into the 1990s, the Matalon name was associated, in Jamaica and throughout the Caribbean, with wealth, success and power. Despite outward appearances, however, a series of developments that began in the mid-1970s were the catalyst for the beginning of the end of that empire. That series of developments resulted in the coming apart of the family business and the breakdown of the family unity that had obtained for over forty years. Just as their father Joseph had predicted, the cards stayed strong while they remained a pack, but apart they were weak and easily torn.

In retrospect, one might date the first catalytic event to June 1975. Aaron and his wife Marjorie were the victims of a hold up at their weekend home in Newcastle. It was a traumatic incident during which Marjorie was injured. While in a larger view it was symptomatic of the dramatic increase in crime and violence that accompanied the social and economic dislocation of the 1970s, at an individual level it caused them great distress and soured them toward Jamaica. They left soon after to live in Miami. Whereas Aaron had hitherto been a strong supporter and proponent of the government's policies, he now considered that violence and the prospect of Cuban-style socialism had brought about a lack of confidence and productivity, and induced a level of hysteria at all levels of society.[5] Like many other Jamaicans, Michael Manley's own daughter included, while they believed in the country that Michael was trying to build, Aaron had grown disenchanted when their comfortable way of life was threatened, and his response—undoubtedly an agonizing decision—was to leave.[6] Though none of the Matalons would have experienced the otherwise general scarcity of consumer goods and food items, and may have been insulated from the frequent power (electricity) cuts, Aaron at least was not spared the violence and fear that characterized life for so many in 1970s Jamaica. Aaron's view after the hold-up was that Michael Manley and the PNP had failed to deliver their promise of a more just and equal society, and instead had ushered in an era of uncontrollable chaos. Aaron faced the moment confronted by many caught up in millenarian movements: the dream was not going to come true.

Not only did Aaron emigrate, he wanted everyone in the family to leave, and tried to convince the other siblings. Vernon, Adele and Gloria left, though Vernon and Aaron continued to commute between Miami, where their families had settled, and Kingston. Over time Aaron came to Jamaica less and less frequently. Owen's family settled in Miami though he was engaged in major infrastructural projects in Trinidad, St. Lucia, St. Kitts and later the Cayman Islands from the 1970s onwards. Eli had suffered a heart attack in 1974, after which ongoing related health problems forced him to resign from government in 1975. He moved to Florida in 1976 ostensibly for medical care, but no doubt the fact that so many of his siblings had relocated there was a draw. Pauline had left Jamaica with Jack some years before. Seven of the ten siblings left Jamaica within a year.

Zackie remained in Morant Bay. Moses and Mayer refused to leave, and resented Aaron's efforts to convince the others to go. As disenchanted as Mayer was with the direction of the government, the increasing crime and violence, and the growing instability, he was not convinced that Jamaica faced any real threat. He did not feel pressured to join the thousands of other Jewish, Chinese and other middle and upper class Jamaicans who participated in an exodus from which, in one view, Jamaica never recovered. (Another view is that their leaving freed Jamaica from the class and color hegemony that those groups represented.) Where those who didn't leave would joke that they were staying "to turn the lights off," Mayer's retort was that he was staying "to supervise the person turning off the lights."[7]

But even as he joked, Mayer was upset by the break up of the family. For thirty years they had worked together, building, literally and figuratively, the family business. Migration weakens families and corrodes social trust. He disagreed not only with his own family's reasons for leaving, but those of the thousands of other Jamaicans who migrated. He was extremely irritated by those who left the country only to criticize it from abroad; to Mayer's mind they should have stayed and worked to get the country to where they wanted it to be. That his own siblings had joined this cadre of dissidents appalled him, as much as how unnecessary he thought their drastic action had been.

When Florizel died in 1979, the family glue came further unstuck, as is often the case with families that are in the process of expanding and dispersing. While external forces are pulling them apart, the matriarch or patriarch is the linchpin holding the family together, and no one realizes this until he or she is gone. Florizel's home was the family's main gathering place, and she the main anchor. Without her, the drift that had begun with the migration of so many family members became an unstoppable current.

Adding to the family tension it caused, Aaron and the others' migration left a managerial void in the business, exacerbated by the simultaneous migration of many of their senior managers. By now, the group of companies had grown so big that without all hands on deck, management of so many different interests became dispersed and weakened. Many of the businesses suffered. There was no option to sell or divest any of the entities because there was no one in Jamaica to buy them. At the same time as the capacity to manage so many businesses had diminished, the family members' ongoing need for support to maintain the lifestyle they were accustomed to in Jamaica brought added financial pressure. Any surplus from the businesses was being diverted to cover their living expenses, and for those who commuted, airfares back and forth. There was nothing to plough back or to fund a reserve to protect the business. Whereas many emigrating Jamaicans started new businesses in the United States and Canada, some quite successful, by this time most of the brothers no longer had the energy and motivation to go down that road. Aaron was approaching sixty and had been working for forty-seven years. Moreover, without each other there was no magic of the triumvirate of Mayer, Aaron and Moses.

Though they were not working day to day in Jamaica, the siblings abroad were still shareholders, and still dependent on income from the company; inevitably there were disagreements over business decisions being taken in Jamaica. Disagreements were nothing new, but the ability to resolve them was far less, at a distance of several hundred miles, than when their offices had been a shouting distance from each other at Harbour Street. All this made for a perfect storm that was the beginning of the conglomerate's eventual demise—and of what would later become a serious family divide.

Mayer stayed at Harbour Street, continuing to manage and grow the businesses where there was scope. He ventured into tourism with the purchase of the Shaw Park Beach Hotel in Ocho Rios, and into the then-new and promising "807" garment assembly sector. He increasingly supported his son Joe M. as he (Joe M.) took the company into new areas. Chief among these new ventures were insurance and financial services. They founded the Industrial Finance Corporation in a joint venture with the Bank of Nova Scotia; they purchased Eagle Star's British Caribbean Insurance Company (BCIC); they founded Sigma Investment Management, a security dealership, and Prime Life Assurance Company. Joe led and implemented these developments, with Mayer's support as chairman and advisor. Some of the siblings' children—those who hadn't migrated to Miami or elsewhere—joined the business, which was still large and diverse enough to find a job for anyone who wanted one, even without specific qualifications or experience.

Mayer also made his own investments: in other people's startups that struck him as having good prospects, in real estate overseas, and in share offerings on the Jamaican stock market and elsewhere. Some of these investments were very lucrative, and his own personal wealth vastly outpaced that of his siblings. Some brothers and their offspring saw Mayer as selfishly looking out for himself and not making investments on behalf of ICD and the family's interests. Mayer was hurt and offended by these accusations; he had often offered investment opportunities to the others but they mostly declined, thinking the ventures too risky. When some of the profitable family businesses were sold, Mayer suggested that rather than distribute all the cash, the lion's share of the proceeds should be pooled as an investment fund to preserve capital and to provide sustained income for the family members. The family members overseas rejected that proposal, though one or two brothers entrusted him to make investments on their behalf, along with his own.

In the 1980s, as WIHCON had fewer large scale housing projects in Jamaica, Moses and Owen embarked on mass housing projects in Trinidad, where they built eighteen thousand homes, and in St. Lucia, where they dredged swamps and reclaimed dozens of acres of land that were later essential to the growing tourism sector. St. Lucia's main seaports, its marina, and a causeway linking the mainland to an old colonial fort were envisioned and created largely by Moses Matalon.[8] Similar projects followed in St. Kitts, after which Moses and Owen went to the Cayman Islands and embarked on the Safe Haven project, a massive golf course development. That project, however, turned out not to be as financially viable as previous ones, and drained resources from WIHCON. The Cayman venture would prove to be a source of conflict between Moses, Owen and Mayer, which would spread through the siblings and their children, adding to the existing discontent.

In the 1980s, as the Jamaican economy began to recuperate, ICD and its subsidiaries, as well as the other non-listed businesses, sought to revive or improve their positions and market share. In so doing they took on debt to finance their operations. Over the years they had invested in a lot of property—land, warehouses, shopping centers—and so their financial surpluses were tied up in real estate, leaving them to borrow the working capital to keep the businesses going. Carrying debt is a normal aspect of many business models, but is difficult to sustain in a context of high and indefinitely rising interest rates. Jamaican financial analysts, commenting on the ICD annual reports, noted this trend from the mid- to late-1980s and speculated on the dilemma that might arise with regard to rising interest rates, foreseeing the need to restructure the debt to restore viability to the businesses.[9] The writing was on the wall.

Independent financial analysts were not the only ones who made these predictions. Mayer's son Joe M. proposed to the family in the mid- to late-1980s that the group enter into a sale and leaseback transaction over all its operating real estate in an effort to substantially reduce debt. Soundings with a number of institutional investors gave every indication that such a transaction would have been well received by the market. While Mayer might have gone along with the proposal, whether because he was partial to it because the idea came from Joe M. or not, the other senior family members insisted that real estate was their best hedge against inflation and currency devaluation.

Some of the manufacturing operations were no longer viable by the 1980s, once imports were liberalized in Jamaica. Without protection from being undercut by cheaper imported goods, many local producers were rendered uncompetitive. One of the first subsidiaries to be closed was the Hosiery Company of Jamaica. Mayer denied that the company was closing because imports were cheaper, arguing that his products were competitive once importers paid the duties due, and alleging that the competition was importing illicitly.[10]

The indebtedness became truly intolerable in the 1990s, when the government began to pursue a monetary policy that led to high and increasing interest rates over a long period of time. At one point, a bank overdraft carried an interest rate as high as 60 percent. The carrying cost of the debt increased dramatically; at the same time the market conditions for many of the ICD and Commodity Services Company businesses had changed, profits had decreased, and in some cases they were making a loss. The turmoil in the Jamaican economy was felt acutely by all the Matalon family businesses, and in turn by the family members who relied on them. The need for a restructuring of the debt and the businesses grew more pressing.

Nevertheless, up to the mid-1990s, between WIHCON and ICD and its subsidiaries, the Matalons were still the largest housing developer in Jamaica; the second largest distributor of food and a main distributor of hardware, pharmaceuticals and other consumer products; and a major provider of insurance, investment management and financial products and services. Facey Commodity, Butterkist Biscuits, Serge Island Dairies, Redimix Concrete, Shoppers Fair Supermarkets, and Homelectrix were all ICD subsidiaries or Matalon-owned companies. These were some of the best-established brands in Jamaica, many of them household names.

Moses passed in 1992, Zackie in 1998. Mayer now proposed a dramatic plan to the remaining siblings and their children to revive the businesses and thereby the family fortunes. Once again, the Matalons would do something innovative, something that had never been done before in Jamaica: a share offering on the New York Stock Exchange to recapitalize the debt. This bold initiative, intended to restore the Matalons and their businesses to the commanding heights of the Jamaican economy, would instead bring about a radical transformation of the business and of the family's role in it.

NOTES

1. "The Matalon Family Success Story: A Living Example to All Jamaicans," *Jamaica Chamber of Commerce Journal* 33, no. 3 (September 1977): 11–13.

2. Stanley Reid, "An Introductory Approach to the Concentration of Power in the Jamaican Corporate Economy and Notes on Its Origin," in *Essays on Power and Change in Jamaica*, ed. Carl Stone and Aggrey Brown (Kingston: Jamaica Publishing House, 1977), 15–44.

3. "The Matalon Family Success Story."

4. Ibid.

5. Ibid.

6. Rachel Manley, *In My Father's Shade: A Daughter's Insight into the Man Behind the Prime Minister's Mask* (Toronto: Alfred Knopf, 2000).

7. Matalon, "Remembrances of Dad."

8. "St. Lucia Names Causeway in Honour of Moses Matalon," *Observer*, August 17, 2015, www.jamaicaobserver.com/news/St-Lucia-names-causeway-in-honour-of-Moses-Matalon_19224144.

9. Carl Aldridge, "Non-Public Companies in the Matalon Group," *Money Index* 325, June 23, 1992, 16.

10. "Hosiery Co. Closing Down," *Gleaner*, September 30, 1988, 1.

Chapter Six

Housing

Of all their business exploits and accomplishments, the area for which the Matalon family is best known in Jamaica is housing. To say that the Matalons revolutionized housing in Jamaica would not be overstating the case.

In the 1950s, while there was a clear need for affordable housing, land and construction costs put a house outside the reach of the majority of Jamaicans. It was the Matalons who, in 1957, came up with a Jamaican version of the system in the United States where a single developer undertook the process of acquiring land and building a house ready for purchase.[1]

The Matalons conceptualized a similar system, adapted to the particularities of the Jamaican housing market and construction capabilities, and taking account of potential natural disasters like hurricanes and earthquakes. To keep costs down the system would be vertically integrated—a sole entity would import the materials, design the houses and do the construction, eliminating the fees and margins that come with employing separate contractors and architects. The designs would be simple and standardized, as would be the titles and contracts. A small down-payment with a twenty-year mortgage would open up home ownership to a much larger section of the population than had previously been the case. Though today these are standard features of the Jamaican housing market, in 1957 they were truly pioneering ideas.

A Puerto Rican construction company, Fullana Brothers, had developed a low-cost housing construction method that was well suited to Jamaica. Led by Mayer Matalon, the Jamaican government was persuaded to sell the company one hundred and fifty acres of government land at Mona, near the University, which had been slated as the site of the capital of the West Indies Federation before it was relocated to Chaguaramas (Trinidad and Tobago). The Matalons' close association with Norman Manley was thought to have helped with the transfer of this property, though they paid above-market rates

Figure 6.1. Image that appeared of Mayer Matalon in LIFE magazine. The original caption was "Jamaican builder Mayer Matalon talking with a tenant of a typical new house." April 01, 1959.
Robert W. Kelley | The LIFE Picture Collection | Getty Images.

for it. It is more likely though that Norman Manley was delighted at the plan, as any leader interested in development would have been.

There was a great deal of skepticism about the project, which at the time seemed audacious and unrealistic. The idea of seven hundred identical houses, side by side, with only a small yard and no fence, was inconceivable in Jamaica. The endeavor did not go smoothly at first. The Matalons were accused in the press and elsewhere of building a "middle class slum right in front of beautiful Hope Gardens,"[2] consisting of matchbox houses that would be washed away in heavy rain. Other land speculators and construction interests opposed the project, and the chairman of the Architects' Association attacked it publicly. The rumors and criticisms led to the cancellation of four hundred-plus purchase agreements. Eventually, due in large part to Aaron Matalon's creative marketing, they all sold (see fig. 6.1).[3]

It was at this time that the Matalons established West Indies Home Contractors (WIHCON) and introduced the "monolithic pour," whereby concrete floors and walls were cast in a continuous mass. The result was Mona Heights: 716 three-bedroom, two-bathroom houses, targeted at civil servants, teachers and professionals who otherwise would have had little if any opportunity to own a new house.

An important element of this project was the mortgage financing, which opened up the market to many new participants. It also marked a turning point in Mayer Matalon's reputation as a financial wizard and expert negotiator. Eagle Star Insurance, one of Britain's largest insurance companies, financed the mortgages, but they had to be persuaded that a company with no previous experience in housing construction, and an unsophisticated and undeveloped financial market, was worth the risk.

To bring this about, Mayer Matalon went to England to persuade Sir Brian Mountain, the principal of Eagle Star, in person—an audacious and novel move for a relative nobody in English terms. Mayer spent months in London, essentially waiting out Mountain's resistance. Eventually Mountain saw him and agreed to the proposal, earning Mayer the nickname "the Baron" from his brothers.

From then on, Brian Mountain, impressed by the young man's persistence and confidence, became a mentor to Mayer Matalon. At one point he tried to hire him to run the Mountain Family Trust out of the Bahamas, but Mayer declined, opting to remain working with his brothers in Jamaica. It was not the first such opportunity Mayer had been offered, but he was committed to the family enterprise. Now in his mid-thirties, the relationship with Mountain would open many doors for Mayer Matalon.

With the success of Mona Heights, the Matalons established a precedent in housing construction. Led by Moses and Owen, adjustments were made to the building system to make it more profitable. With Aaron, Mayer Matalon undertook virtually every administrative aspect of the projects, from planning and logistics, to working directly with their legal team from Myers, Fletcher and Gordon—where Mayer first met Pat Rousseau—to marketing and sales.

After Mona Heights, the "WIHCON system" was refined and customized, both technically and as related to skilled workers. A succession of WIHCON projects followed: one thousand eight hundred homes targeted at low income families in Harbour View; then another low-income housing scheme of two thousand three hundred two-bedroom homes in Duhaney Park; and across from Harbour View, a smaller, seventy-four-house scheme in Caribbean Terrace. The Hughenden Park scheme in 1967 was an aesthetic breakthrough. Its six hundred houses were the most attractive scheme homes yet, breaking the previous mold of plain, no-frills units. Then in 1969, came Independence City (fig. 6.2), the first large housing scheme in Portmore, comprising over a thousand two- and three-bedroom houses. The building of this scheme marked the beginning of Kingston's expansion into Portmore, inarguably one of the most important urban developments in Jamaica since independence.

WIHCON's housing projects spawned numerous subsidiary businesses as part of a vertically integrated operation to keep costs down: Caribbean Brush

Figure 6.2. Independence City housing scheme construction site, March 9, 1968. The Prime Minister, the Hon. Hugh Shearer (second, left) talks with Mayer Matalon, in his capacity as chairman of West Indies Home Contractors. Others in the group (from left, front) are: the Hon. Wilton Hill, Minister of Housing; the Hon. Victor Grant, Minister of Legal Affairs (M.P. for the Area); Mr. Warren Wolff, A. I. D. investment officer; Mr. Lloyd Collins, Permanent Secretary, Ministry of Housing. At the rear are Mr. Richard Ware, head of A. I. D. in Jamaica; Mr. Walter Tobriner, American Ambassador; and Mr. Robert Montgomery, managing director of Jamaica National Mortgage Association Ltd., developers of the scheme.
Courtesy of the Gleaner Company (Media) Limited

Company, Tropicair Jalousies (windows manufacturers), West Indies Paints, Redimix (concrete manufacturers), and Painters and Decorators Limited. The company was organized in such a way as to maximize the individual brothers' skills: while Aaron was responsible for the vision and marketing of the developments, Mayer was the financial brain. He negotiated with the government to secure the tracts of land, and sourced and managed financing. Owen and Moses conceptualized the engineering and technical aspects, working on the ground and in the day-to-day operations of WIHCON and its subsidiary, Construction and Dredging. Nor were they inward-looking: Owen and Moses garnered ideas, for example, from Israel, where mass housing construction was state of the art. The unique prefabricated construction system they developed for WIHCON became a model for other Jamaican developers and gained international attention.

With Mayer as deal-maker, WIHCON built houses in Trinidad in the 1980s, and in the late 1990s went as far as Nigeria, where Mayer negotiated with the interim Abubakar government to build ten thousand houses, the biggest housing contract ever awarded anywhere. After months of travel, negotiations and paperwork, just as Mayer and his team were heading to Abuja to finalize the signing, they were stopped in their tracks. After a year in office, Abubakar had handed over power to the new democratically elected president General Olusegun Obasanjo, and all government contracts were cancelled.

At home in Jamaica, however, the Matalons' housing initiatives were unparalleled, as illustrated by the Portmore development in 1969. Before the Matalon project, the population of Portmore was two thousand; in 2012, the census counted one hundred eighty-two thousand people (though some contend the figure is closer to three hundred thousand).[4] Housing constitutes one of the most significant advances in Jamaica in the twentieth century. By putting a roof over the heads of thousands of families and providing thousands of jobs, the Matalons provided access to the most significant asset most people would own in their lifetime. From being known to the elite as illustrious members of the business class, the Matalon name became a household word among ordinary Jamaicans.

Their success was not, however, without controversy and misunderstanding, as these examples from Jamaican popular culture will show. From the very outset of the Matalon family's rise to prominence, the Matalon name featured in popular discourse:

> As a small boy growing up in Jamaica. . . . I remember well that we used to chant as we walked down King Street, which was then a fashionable street of elegant department stores:
> Ashes to ashes, dust to dust
> If Issa don't get you, Matalon must.
> [The chant] reflected the reality that despite the different stores with their different names, they were all owned by Issa Brothers enterprises or Matalon Brothers enterprises.[5]

What is interesting about this passage, taken from a presentation by Franklyn Knight, a prominent Jamaican historian at Johns Hopkins University, is that at the time that he recalls this being a popular ditty, in the early 1950s, the Matalon Brothers did not own more than one store on King Street (Matalon Brothers, the dry goods business that Joseph had started and Aaron had continued). Those were still the early years of the family's business, and department stores on King Street were not among their ventures then. Others recall the ditty having originated in a pantomime, being recited more in the 1960s and 1970s, which would be a more accurate chronology, (and with a slightly different wording: "if the Issas don't get you, the Matalons must"). The perception of the Matalons' wealth and the extent of their reach was so deeply ingrained in the minds of so many Jamaicans, no doubt entrenched by their name having been on the "21 families" list, that it belied accurate recollections of the details behind that perception.

Those misperceptions endured over the decades, and featured in popular culture. The 1996 hit song by Anthony B., "Fire Pon' Rome," an anti-establishment polemic, articulated grass-roots resentment toward Jamaica's business and political elites. Alongside attacks on former prime ministers, P. J. Patterson and Edward Seaga, and yet-to-be prime minister, Bruce Golding, the song named the Issas (another prominent Lebanese-Jamaican family who were significant players in the Jamaican hotel industry), Butch Stewart (a white Jamaican hotelier and one of Jamaica's best-known businessmen since the 1980s), and, referring to their housing developments—"Check out greater Portmore, Braeton; One room unno build a sell fi one million"—the Matalons:

[. . .] and the one Matalon
How unno get fi own so much black people land?

A 2011 song, "Poor People Land," by one of the most popular Jamaican artistes in the early 2000s, Vybz Kartel, echoed those sentiments, with lyrics essentially accusing the Matalons (though most likely referring to them by name insofar as "Matalon" represented the wealthy developer class), of obtaining land unfairly, and of not being really Jamaican:

Somebody tell me weh Matalon come from?
Fi own so much inna wi island.[6]

Despite similar popular misrepresentations over the years Mayer remained unruffled.

The references to land and Portmore are significant, if misunderstood. In 1966 the Matalons, led by Moses, approached the government with a plan to build a causeway (a road connecting two points across a broad expanse of water or wetland) across the Kingston Harbor, so as to develop two thousand acres of swamp as a new residential area near Port Henderson, in Kingston's neighboring parish of St. Catherine. With a growing population and no more space for large-scale housing developments, Kingston was squeezed.[7] The proposal to build a causeway and drain the swamps was groundbreaking—in every sense of the word. In the twenty-first century we take modern engineering for granted; in the 1960s these were radical propositions with far-reaching consequences for the development of Jamaica's capital city.

Through two new companies, Construction and Dredging, and Foreshore Development Company, the Matalons went on to create a deep-water port in the Kingston Harbor, reclaiming a part of the Kingston shoreline to create Newport East and West, which became modern port facilities that accommodated large ships.[8] These innovations were key to Jamaica's positioning as a major trans-shipment port. Furthermore, Moses, as head of the Urban Development Corporation (UDC), opened up the potential for tourism by spearheading the reclamation of dozens of acres of beach land and the dredging of the harbor in Ocho Rios; through these measures, Ocho Rios went on to become one of Jamaica's most significant tourism centers. Moses and Owen, often with Mayer negotiating the deals, performed similar feats in St. Lucia, St. Kitts and the Cayman Islands.

When WIHCON created a plan to build over ten thousand houses in Greater Portmore in the early 1990s, it was one of the largest development projects ever undertaken in Jamaica or the English-speaking Caribbean. It was also a hallmark of all that Mayer Matalon had brought about through his financial expertise, his contacts in government, and his ability to bring many disparate players together to realize an ambitious vision. The San Jose Accord of 1980 provided for credit and concessionary prices on Venezuelan and Mexican oil to Central American and Caribbean countries, and was also a vehicle for the funding of development projects in the receiving countries. Mayer persuaded Michael Manley to propose to the Venezuelan and Mexican governments that a housing scheme represented an appropriate use of the funds from the Accord.[9] Only someone with the type of relationship Mayer had with Manley could have convinced the prime minister to pursue using the funds in this unorthodox way. Mayer proposed that the government role should be to provide the land and import the equipment and materials as part of a complex public-private partnership. Again, only someone with Mayer's wide range of contacts and relationships, many of them, by this time, decades-old, would have had the capacity to bring so many ostensibly unconnected elements together and make them work. The demand for the houses that resulted was so intense that there was nearly a stampede at the National Arena when applications opened.[10]

Perhaps Mayer Matalon's most ingenious financial solution in the area of housing was his conceptualization of the National Housing Trust (NHT), a hallmark initiative to assist more Jamaicans to own homes through low-cost mortgages. The idea combined many of his interests and affinities. With nearly two decades of experience in the building and financing of mass housing projects, he understood every aspect of housing development. He had long been concerned about the problem of lack of housing for poor Jamaicans, and he believed that if the state could assist in providing them with affordable housing, it would inculcate a sense of social responsibility in Jamaicans that would do much for future social cohesion.[11]

Mayer envisioned a government mortgage provider that would provide far broader access to home loan financing than any private financial institution in a developing country like Jamaica. Given the foreign exchange volatility and general instability of the 1970s, funding for large-scale housing development could not be reliably sourced from overseas. Housing projects therefore required a local source of funding. The more lower and middle-income individuals and families had access to mortgages, the more houses could be built.

Mayer Matalon suggested the idea of the National Housing Trust to Michael Manley in 1974. He obtained the legislation for a similar type of state mortgage entity from Mexico, had it translated into English, and submitted it to Manley. From there Manley developed the idea of an employee and employer-funded pool to provide low-interest mortgages for the purchase or building of homes. The NHT also did its own housing developments; its first, a community of two-bedroom homes in the "Portmore Area"—Portmore had not yet been developed into the many different communities and neighborhoods it later became—was built by WIHCON.

The costs, scope and risk of the large mass housing construction projects were extraordinary for a small developing country like Jamaica. Mayer brought inventiveness and creativity to WIHCON's endeavors in this field, doing the background work that enabled the Matalons' vision to become walls, roofs and homes for thousands of Jamaicans. The Greater Portmore project was the last of WIHCON's large housing schemes; by then, other entities had entered the mass housing market in Jamaica, with their own low-cost building systems. But the Matalons were the first.

NOTES

1. "History: WIHCON History Formative Years 1959–1963," WIHCON website, 2017, www.wihcon.com/history.

2. Ferguson, "The Growth of an Empire."

3. Ibid.

4. Ingrid Brown, "Mayor Says Close to 300,000 Living in Portmore, Not 182,000," *Observer*, June 18, 2013, www.jamaicaobserver.com/news/Census-wrong_14519318.

5. Franklyn W. Knight, "The Crisis in the Contemporary Caribbean," *Contributions in Black Studies* 6, no. 2 (2008), www.scholarworks.umass.edu/cibs/vol6/iss1/2.

6. Translation: Check out greater Portmore, Braeton (both are large housing developments in St. Catherine); you build a one-room house and sell it for one million dollars. [With regard to] the said Matalon, how did you come to own so much of black people's land?

7. "History of Portmore," National Library of Jamaica website, 2015, www.nlj.gov.jm/history-notes/History%20of%20Portmore%20Final.pdf.

8. "Business: Another Matalon Milestone," *Newday* 7, no. 3 (March, 1963).

9. "History: High Point 1991–2001," WIHCON website, 2017, www.wihcon.com/history.

10. "A Very Expensive Low-Cost Housing Scheme," *Gleaner*, January 21, 1989, 24.

11. "There Are No Rights without Corresponding Responsibilities, Sir Neville Tells JC Boys," *Gleaner*, August 8, 1967, 23.

Chapter Seven

On the Inside of Political Decision Making, 1950–2010

We make no secret of our politics—we belong to the PNP. We feel it is our duty to support one or the other of the island's two political parties.

Aaron Matalon, 1963.[1]

Between the free-enterprise system and communism one seeks to find a middle road, and I believe that particularly in the underdeveloped world, the mixed economy of public and private sector is the only solution to creating the speed of development necessary to improve the welfare of the mass of the population.

Mayer Matalon, 1976.[2]

As well known for their politics as they were for their innovations in business and housing, from as early as 1946 the Matalon brothers were proud and committed supporters of the People's National Party (PNP). It was strikingly notable for members of the business and merchant class to support the PNP, and even more so given that they were Jewish.[3] But the Matalons, though white, Jewish and in business, in the 1940s and 1950s did not have property to defend. Coming, as they did, from owning nothing, and not being part of the establishment, they had no political or financial legacy to uphold, so they were free to follow a different political path. Furthermore, their progressive business and entrepreneurial outlook extended to their political vision for Jamaica. They saw the PNP as the originator of independence and nationhood, ideals they also upheld.

The older Matalon brothers, from Zackie to Mayer, forged close relationships with Florizel Glasspole and Norman Manley, among others. Though Mayer was his son Michael's schoolmate, Norman Manley recognized his financial acumen and his capacity for hard work, and brought him in as an advisor on investment and economic policy. Mayer often accompanied Norman Manley on trips to England to consult on matters related to the West Indies Federation, and thereafter, independence.

After Zackie moved to St. Thomas to manage his wife's family's farm, he ran for a PNP seat in the House of Representatives in the 1959 and 1962 elections. Though he was unsuccessful both times, he was later appointed to Jamaica's first Senate, after which he served as custos of St. Thomas for twenty years, until shortly before he died in 1998. Zackie is regarded as having laid the early foundations for the PNP in St. Thomas, a parish with a long history of JLP allegiance on the sugar estates in Duckenfield and Serge Island, where Bustamante held sway over politics and the unions.

More broadly, the Matalons' support of the PNP helped to open up a degree of corporate support for the party, at a time when the business establishment was suspicious of it. At the same time, the Matalons mitigated the PNP's own hostility to the private sector by proving themselves loyal and committed to the party.

Despite their ties to the PNP, the Matalon brothers were known by politicians and observers on all sides of the Jamaican political spectrum as, first and foremost, Jamaican nationalists. Their thinking may have been aligned with the PNP's but Mayer, especially, never let his political leanings come before his service to the country. This nationalist loyalty was both sentimental and practical, as the Matalons—and other entrepreneurs of that era, and since—knew that a prosperous and stable Jamaica was the most desirable environment for their business interests. It was only appropriate, therefore, to do whatever they could to contribute to, and ensure, prosperity and stability, regardless of the party in power.

The Matalons were, therefore, careful to maintain at least the appearance of a balance in their political donations. To this end, for many years Mayer collaborated with Carlton Alexander, head of GraceKennedy, Jamaica's largest company at the time, in matching their political contributions.

At a more fundamental level, the Matalons, in particular Mayer, worked closely with, advised and served senior politicians and prime ministers in both parties. Mayer Matalon's strongest and deepest relationship was with Michael Manley, but after Manley's retirement he worked closely with Omar Davies, finance minister in the successive PNP governments of 1993–2007. But while he was known as a "PNP man," and never denied that ascription, throughout his life he was advisor to, and in some cases friends with, JLP prime ministers, from JLP founder and Jamaica's first prime minister, Alexander Bustamante, to his successors, Hugh Shearer, Edward Seaga, and Bruce Golding. He enjoyed the confidence of both PNP and JLP leadership over the years that he would always act and give advice that was in the best interests of the nation.

Mayer valued being party to decision making at the very highest level for two reasons. In the first place, it gave him access to important information to which few others had access, and secondly, he was happiest when he was in a position of power. Though he successfully courted and maintained relationships with powerful people throughout his life, it was not his way to push himself forward; he always waited to be summoned. His object was not fame for he was extremely discreet, but for the satisfaction of knowing that his opinion mattered and that he exerted an impact on important decisions and actions. As a close friend remarked, he suffered withdrawal symptoms if he wasn't in a position of influence.

For their part, politicians sought his expertise, advice and contacts, and considered the flourishing of the Matalons' businesses to be as much in the nation's interest as their own. When the approval of their Hughenden housing scheme was announced in Parliament in 1967, it was reported that PNP MP, Wills Isaacs, "laughed at the [JLP] Government for being so dependent on these developers now, as oppose[d] to when the present Opposition was the Government and was criticized for being closely linked with the same Matalons; now the Matalons have taken over the Government party and soul." Prime Minister Bustamante stated in response, "I don't think it's in the best interests of the country to keep the Matalons in the doghouse. If they have schemes which can benefit the country we shouldn't make it difficult for them. I wish they were members of our party though."[4] Indeed, one of Bustamante's first projects as prime minister was to support the Matalon-led transformation of the Kingston waterfront. Norman Manley, as chief minister, had not approved it, but Bustamante saw the prospects of developing the waterfront and creating the wharf, a project that ultimately led to the creation of the industrial estates at Newport East and Newport West. It is said that Busta told Moses, who had led the charge on this initiative, "I like you even though I know you are a Communist."[5] Aaron and Busta also enjoyed a close relationship dating back before 1945.[6]

Mayer's influence was exerted mostly behind the scenes; those instances that we know of indicate the extent of his reach and effect. Between Norman Manley and Alexander Bustamante, Mayer was given the mission in 1961–1962 to negotiate with the British over the sale of the War Department lands at Up Park Camp. Before independence, Up Park Camp was the seat of the British military, as it would be for the newly formed Jamaica Defence Force upon independence. Leading up to independence, however, the British War Department had a land agent on the island advertising land for sale and carrying out sales and conveyancing. Up Park Camp was offered to the new

Jamaican government at a very high price. Bustamante's position, it was said, was that he was not paying all that money, so the British were to "take up the land and go with it."[7]

As this was clearly impractical, negotiations ensued and the forty-year-old Mayer was dispatched to London. On arrival, he commissioned a freelance journalist to write a story that was sympathetic to Jamaica, and which portrayed the British government as extortionist and unreasonable. When Mayer met with the state minister in the War Office he presented the draft news story to him, saying someone had sent it to him. He suggested to the minister that, should the UK government maintain their position with regard to the price of the land, the resulting news story would be very unflattering. Shortly after that meeting the United Kingdom came back with an offer to sell the land to the Jamaican government at what was effectively a peppercorn price.

Behind the scenes, Bustamante assisted the Matalons when political obstacles got in their way. A rough agreement as to how the labor force would be organized on the Matalons' construction projects had been struck between Busta and his Bustamante Industrial Trade Union (BITU), the JLP's workers' union, and Florizel Glasspole of the PNP's National Workers' Union (NWU). The party-in-power's people would get 60 percent of the jobs and the opposition's would get 40 percent. This formula worked well for the construction of Mona and Harbour View, and throughout the following decades of the Matalons' massive housing projects. It was key to the lack of labor disruptions on their sites. But when they started on the Duhaney Park housing scheme, Clem Tavares, JLP minister of labor, wanted all the jobs for his people and brought in henchmen to invade the site.

Mayer went to Bustamante to complain. While in his office, Bustamante said he would deal with Tavares. As Mayer got up to leave, Bustamante instructed him to stay in the room. He called in Gladys Longbridge (then his secretary, later his wife) and dictated a brusque letter to Tavares telling him to stop interfering or he would no longer be minister. Tavares in turn had to go back to Mayer to ask him to get Bustamante off his case.

On a personal level, Bustamante was friendly with and fond of the Matalon brothers; he particularly enjoyed Mayer's wit and sense of humor, and admired his business sense. When there was a fire at Mayer's home on Seymour Avenue (no one was injured), Busta called Mayer, who was in London at the time, and joked, "Man you smart, you make sure you bun' it down when you not here!"[8]

Of all Mayer Matalon's ties to power, none surpassed his relationship with Michael Manley, Jamaica's prime minister, 1972–1980, and again 1989–1992. Whereas his work with Norman Manley and Hugh Shearer entailed advising on financial, economic and investment related matters, Mayer's relationship with Michael Manley went beyond that. They had been friends since Jamaica College, where Michael was Mayer's "fag"—an adopted British public school custom whereby a younger boy did personal services and ran errands for an older one. As a result, Mayer Matalon was one of Michael Manley's most trusted advisors and closest confidantes. Mayer had license to remind Michael, even in the presence of others, of his being his fag, and tell him to mind himself accordingly. When Michael would get animated or wax poetic in a political discussion or argument, Mayer would jokingly rein him in with, "All right Laurence Olivier, we don't need an act today. Just come down to earth."[9]

Though Manley came to power promising change in 1972, Mayer Matalon recognized that Jamaica was changing long before. As a schoolboy he had been witness to the first sparks of change in the labor riots of 1938. Having been in the front row of the negotiations for independence as advisor to Norman Manley, he was at the heart of the intellectual and philosophical debates leading up to and surrounding it. The mood of the country after 1962 was exuberant and positive; a huge energy had been released, and everyone wanted to be part of building a new society and economy. New businesses were launched and local and foreign investments brought about the highest post-independence economic growth rates that Jamaica had ever experienced.

The zeitgeist of the 1962–1972 decade was captured by Prime Minister Hugh Shearer, in his New Year message of 1970 (*inter alia*):

> It [1960–1970] has been a ten-year period of adventurous and spectacular activities, sensational achievements and remarkable progress in Jamaica.
>
> Independence has released new energy and new ambitions. We have moved forward rapidly and are well on our way to our targets.
>
> The year (1969) has been remarkable in the rapid growth rate of our economic development. The New Deal education programme, which aims at providing for education for all Jamaicans, began to take shape and form. Tourism aimed at higher targets and methods. Industrial encouragement received enthusiastic response from local and overseas investors.
>
> There was a national determination to share comfort and prosperity, increased awareness by more individuals and more organizations to involve themselves in social services to the people, and in efforts to bring all Jamaicans into the stream of progress. Most of all, there was an air of urgency which pre-destined a more active involvement in the nation building programme.[10]

The Matalons clearly shared the enthusiasm Shearer referred to, evidenced by their investments in Jamaica during the 1960s. At the same time, there was a recognition among most Jamaicans that the remaining vestiges of the colonial social order needed to be dismantled. Color prejudice, for example, was still entrenched, with opportunity—social, economic, educational—favoring white and fair-skinned Jamaicans. In 1968, Mayer Matalon commented publicly on the changing pattern of society and the changing needs of Jamaica, at the same time bemoaning the lack of a corresponding change in the pattern of education.

The 1970s, particularly 1972–1980 when the PNP was in office, were the most politically, socially and economically turbulent years in the history of modern Jamaica. After enslavement and emancipation, it was arguably *the* defining period for Jamaica, socially, economically and politically. In 1972 the entire country was behind Manley in wanting change. Almost all Jamaicans wanted to bring about a more equitable, balanced and orderly society. It was a pivotal and paradoxical period in independent Jamaica's social and economic trajectory, with gains and losses that are impossible to reconcile. Forty years later, Jamaicans continue to debate the meaning and effects of the 1970s, which are still a flashpoint at all levels.

At the outset of the PNP's time in office in 1972, Mayer Matalon's political philosophy was close to Michael Manley's. He did not consider himself a socialist, but rather preferred to be described as a capitalist with a social conscience. He recognized a context of high unemployment was inimical to social order, and believed a purely free-enterprise system to be inadequate to create the required job opportunities. The cynical view was that Manley's attempts to secure state participation and partnership in the commanding heights of the economy met with full approval of the business class because there were no threats posed to their own interests; and further, almost every state board was populated by PNP businessmen.

Aside from his official title as Ambassador for Special Missions, which was framed broadly enough to cover the various official assignments he carried out on the government's behalf, Mayer Matalon was engaged in ongoing dialogue with Manley over virtually every aspect of government policy, but particularly financial. (Eli Matalon was also close to Michael Manley; besides joining the government, he was godfather to Michael and Beverley's daughter, Natasha.) While their political relationship was underpinned by their strong friendship and shared history, Michael was also influenced by his own father's trust in Mayer. His naiveté about financial issues led him to seek guidance from someone who understood and could operate in local and international financial systems.

The early days of Michael Manley's government were heady and exciting. Middle and even upper class Jamaicans, wanting to be a part of Jamaica's transformation, volunteered in the National Literacy Programme, put themselves forward for parish council seats, and exuberantly jumped into public life wherever they could. Mayer supported the initial steps the government took toward nationalization, such as the acquisition of the Jamaica Omnibus Service Company Limited (public transportation), and the Jamaica Public Service Company (electricity generation and distribution). It was he who gave Manley the idea of the National Housing Trust. When Barclays Bank pulled out of Jamaica in 1975 because economic upheaval was affecting their profitability, Mayer Matalon led the negotiations for the Jamaican government to buy the bank, which then became the National Commercial Bank.

It was in the position of trusted advisor that Mayer Matalon led the Jamaican government's landmark negotiations over the bauxite levy in 1974. Aluminum ore had been discovered in the red dirt of Jamaica's mountains in the early 1940s, and with an increasing demand from North America for its use in construction and machinery, a valuable natural resource lay literally under Jamaica's feet. "Red gold" it was called at the time. In the 1950s and 1960s, Jamaica entered into agreements with several North American bauxite and alumina firms with the technology and capital to invest in mining and processing. From 1957 to 1971, Jamaica was the world's number one bauxite producer.[11]

For Michael Manley's government, renegotiating the terms of the agreements with Reynolds Metals, Kaiser Aluminum, Alcoa, Alcan, Revere and Anaconda—among these were four of the six largest aluminum companies in the world at the time—was a priority. While the PNP was still in opposition they had discussed and analyzed the matter extensively. Jamaica was earning little revenue from the agreements, which were codified under a 1950 law that provided for generous taxation arrangements for the companies, but relatively small royalty payments on mined bauxite. Beyond the money, however, there was a broader principle of sovereignty over Jamaica's natural resources. The agreements, made when Jamaica was still a colony, were precisely the type of shackles that independence had promised to throw off. Though newly independent and in the midst of a swell of populist nationalism, this assertion of sovereignty was a bold move for a small, undeveloped country. It resonated far beyond Jamaica, with other newly independent former colonies, as well as with the multinational corporations that they regarded as their exploiters.[12]

Soon after the election, Michael Manley asked Mayer to chair the newly created Jamaica Bauxite Commission. He did so for a year but gave over the chair to his friend, the lawyer Pat Rousseau, because one of his own overseas business partners was considering investing in bauxite and alumina and he wanted to avoid a conflict of interest. (That business partner did not end up investing in Jamaica's bauxite industry.)

The Jamaica Bauxite Commission team included Sir Egerton Richardson, Jamaica's ambassador to the United States, Horace Barber, financial secretary, and Alister McIntyre, an academic and economist. Carlton Davis, who would go on to become Jamaica's longest serving cabinet secretary, and who later wrote a number of books about the Jamaican bauxite industry, and others, was also on the broader team that provided administrative, research and logistical support. Mayer was acknowledged as the intellectual leader of the team.

While they were researching and analyzing the industry and formulating Jamaica's position in preparation for the negotiations, the country was hit with the 1973 global oil crisis. This was the first major economic shock to Jamaica and precipitated a fiscal crisis when the country's oil bill tripled virtually overnight, causing foreign exchange reserves to go into sharp decline. The objectives of the commission and of the negotiations—to restore bauxite land ownership to Jamaica (the bauxite companies having acquired huge acreages of land over the previous decade and a half), to increase Jamaican government participation in the companies, and to levy a tax on the ore mined—became more than principled positions. They were now immediate needs, essential to resolving the Manley government's desperate shortage of foreign exchange.

The two months of intense negotiations that ensued were a landmark in the history of such international negotiations, especially between a developing country and a multinational corporation. Mayer's insight and capacity to understand the numbers impressed everyone on both sides.

The Jamaican position was that only a small percentage of the bauxite companies' gross profits were being paid to Jamaica in tax, and, the original agreement notwithstanding, the terms should be changed and a mining levy imposed to make the deal more equitable. The levy that was proposed and accepted was significant for many reasons, not least that a small developing country was standing up to large and powerful multinational corporations, and it was supported with a unanimous vote in Parliament.

The US government was unhappy with the move and expressed the same. The negotiations stirred up tension between the United States and Jamaica in an era of US intervention in other countries in its backyard over similar policies and actions of what the United States considered expropriation of its assets; recall Chile, September 1973. The bauxite companies were also pressuring the State Department to defend their interests, though the State Department claimed its interest in the negotiations only went so far as protecting US consumers. Jamaica took pains to manage the Jamaica-US relationship as best as they could alongside the negotiations, and Mayer was the linchpin in the discussions that may have precluded, as Manley put it, "the shadow of a US Marine."[13]

Lawrence "Larry" Eagleburger was US Secretary of State Henry Kissinger's executive assistant. In that job, he was essentially responsible for running the State Department, which during the Watergate period effectively ran America's foreign policy for a distracted White House. He was one of the main people who helped shape US policy on Jamaica.[14] Mayer forged a relationship with Eagleburger as, on behalf of Jamaica, he undertook the explanations and negotiations that became necessary to maintain an even keel with the United States during the negotiations. Together they organized for Manley to speak directly to US Secretary of State Henry Kissinger.

This relationship was a prime example of Mayer's incredible ability to form connections with key people of influence. His association with Eagleburger outlasted these initial encounters and was very helpful to Jamaica in future discussions at State. Through this relationship and his enormous knowledge of the issues, Mayer personally sought to contain any possible adverse reactions from the US government then and later.

The success of the bauxite levy proposal, though on the face of it not a problem for the United States, set the tone for a sour relationship between Jamaica—Michael Manley in particular—and the United States in the years to come, which worsened when Jamaica supported Cuba's assistance to the Angolans in their own anti-colonial struggle. Again Mayer was the channel between the highest levels of the Jamaican government and the State Department when anti-American sentiment on the island heated up and the US ambassador was convinced that Manley had made "a definite flip to the Left."[15]

Mayer Matalon was by now fifty-two years old and at his peak. His performance in the bauxite negotiations cemented his legacy as a financial wizard and a fine business mind. The pace at which he did calculations in his head and his capacity for detail were nothing less than dazzling.

By 1976, however, Mayer began to have concerns about the direction of the government and the country. While he accepted that the change the government was aiming for could only be achieved at the expense of some social upheaval, he feared that the PNP leadership had lost control of the ability to manage the pace. He realized that there were limits on what was possible. His concerns were no doubt influenced by the hold-up and attack on his brother Aaron and Aaron's wife, Marjorie. In a speech in 1976 he said as much:

> I feel that some of the changes have been carried through too rapidly, and that the Government has been carried away by the very human desire of wishing to create the better life for the mass of population as quickly as possible; and in so doing are likely to be faced with the failure of well conceived plans because adequate management was not available.[16]

Privately, he expressed much stronger disagreement with Michael Manley. He was, for example, unhappy with how the money from the bauxite levy was being spent. The original stated intention was that the levy proceeds would fund capital expenditure toward increasing the country's productive capacity, and, after the 1973 oil shocks, provide a buffer against future foreign exchange shortages. But the proceeds, in the view of Mayer Matalon and most of the members of the negotiating team, were misspent on public sector salary increases and other recurring expenditures. When Michael Manley announced free education and increased salaries for civil servants, Mayer complained to Michael that it was "fiscal profligacy."[17] He grew frustrated with Manley when, in trying to calm the Americans and their nervousness about Manley aligning himself with the radical pro-Communist Left, Michael avoided meeting with Mayer to discuss the issues at hand and continued to make public pronouncements that served to confirm US fears.

As the 1970s progressed, Mayer disagreed with Michael more than he agreed with him. The year 1977 was terrible for Jamaica. For the 1976 election, the PNP government undertook massive spending on water, rural electrification, and feeder roads. They had extremely qualified people in the field, including Michael's personal staff, reporting back every day to ensure that things got done. This led, inevitably, to a massive fiscal deficit. Horace Barber, the financial secretary, and G. Arthur Brown, the Central Bank governor, negotiated an IMF loan on condition that the dollar be devalued by 40 percent, but this was kept secret so as not to affect the election.

This move was vehemently opposed by the PNP Left, under pressure from whom Michael eventually buckled and abandoned the agreement. Mayer had not approved of the overspending that brought the need for the agreement about, but disagreed with the decision to break with the IMF and told Michael so, but Michael persisted.

All along, within the PNP, many in the party leadership were suspicious of Mayer and resented his closeness to Michael; they felt he had too much influence on Michael's thinking and decisions, and that his interests were at odds with theirs. The Abeng group within the PNP "identified a clique running things in the government: Mayer Matalon, Eli Matalon, Moses Matalon . . . Manley had surrounded himself with 'these arch-enemies of the people.'"[18] People on the inside of the PNP knew well that if Michael saw Mayer after a matter was settled, and that matter was discussed with Mayer, the matter was no longer settled. Their animus toward Mayer was not only personal but reflective of their more general desire to diminish the role of the class they perceived Mayer as representing, which they felt had dominated decision making and the economy for too long.

Mayer increasingly saw that the PNP's policies and political rhetoric were creating deep divisions in Jamaican society; these divisions came to be replicated in Mayer and Michael's relationship. Mayer grew more and more chagrined as Michael was no longer taking his advice and was letting others in the party change his mind on positions that Mayer had advised him to take.

The decision to abandon the IMF agreement was a critical juncture in Mayer and Michael's relationship and in Mayer's involvement in government policy and decisions in the 1970s. Mayer remained Michael's friend, but he withdrew from seeking to influence policy.[19] This, together with the pushback Michael faced within the party (in some cases specific to Mayer and his influence), meant their relationship inevitably cooled.

The breach in their relationship, particularly from Mayer's end, was no doubt complicated by the situation within his own family. Indeed the relationship with Michael Manley, and the outcomes of the PNP's policies and actions in office in the 1970s, precipitated a profound paradox for Mayer Matalon. On the one hand, this was the period during which he made perhaps his two most significant contributions to Jamaican public policy: his leadership of the bauxite levy negotiations and the idea of the National Housing Trust. On the other, it was also the period during which the PNP's politics and economic policies so changed Jamaica that the thriving Jewish minority evaporated, and with it the community that sustained its members, including his own family; a community that was particularly precious to his wife, Sarita.

Already a tiny community of some 1,500–2,000 people before 1972, by 1978 there were fewer than four hundred Jews in Jamaica. Regardless of whether or not the increase in emigration from Jamaica was a direct outcome of the PNP's social and economic policies—the conventional wisdom being that the economic crisis and redistributive policies were the push factors—the fact was that the Jewish community was decimated. Sarita, a devout, practicing Jew who kept a Jewish household, no longer saw a future for her family in Jamaica. She developed an intense dislike—hatred, according to her daughters—for Michael Manley; to her mind, he had destroyed her world. Mayer was well aware of her view; Sarita, he would say, was "entitled to her opinion."[20]

But it could not have been a small matter to him that from that point on Sarita prepared their daughters to leave Jamaica, to marry Jewish men from countries where they could live the Jewish life that was so precious to her. And so it was. The daughters all left Jamaica after high school, married Panamian Jews ("my Panamaniacs," as Mayer called them), and settled outside Jamaica. They maintained Jewish households and were active participants in the Jewish communities in Panama and Mexico, where they lived. Sarita even offered to help her sisters-in-law find Jewish spouses for their sons and daughters (apparently no one took her up on the offer, as no such match was made).

During this time, Mayer's own brothers and sisters joined the thousands of other middle and upper middle class Jamaicans in migrating, a move that devastated Mayer and was the beginning of an irreparable rift in his own family. The Jamaican economy went into a tailspin that had repercussions on the

Matalons' own businesses at the same time as many of their top managers, the brothers above all, were leaving the island.

After the 1980 election, which brought the JLP—forthrightly capitalist in orientation and determinedly aligned with the United States—to power, the friendship and working relationship between Mayer Matalon and Michael Manley were restored. Where many people abandoned Michael Manley after 1980—as Michael's daughter Rachel later wrote, "the time his country simply ignored him and he picked up the pieces of his life with quiet dignity,"[21]— Mayer stood by him and played a crucial role in helping Manley and the PNP at many levels. It is openly acknowledged that Manley left office penniless; it was Mayer who quietly helped to support him and his family in the early 1980s. Mayer also kept the party financially afloat, paying the salaries of the office staff and providing the ongoing expenditure necessary for the PNP to maintain its institutional framework and remain a viable political party.

As Michael began to analyze the policy errors of the 1970s and listen to more moderate views, Mayer Matalon's were chief among them. Officially he was on the party's economic commission, advising the PNP's shadow cabinet on finance and economic policy. Privately, as before, he was Michael's principal sounding board. Through this process of analysis and discussion, in which Mayer was a key participant and driver, significant changes were made to what had been accepted PNP policy in the seventies. As Michael Manley and the PNP underwent a shift in their approach to development policy and strategy, Mayer helped Manley repair many of the relationships fractured during the 1970s, even with people Mayer himself was at odds with.

His critical role in keeping the PNP alive in the 1980s and in rehabilitating Michael Manley so he could return to power in 1989, did not prevent Mayer from also working with and advising Edward Seaga, prime minister in the JLP administration of 1980–1989. Though they were not well acquainted before 1980, and they never enjoyed a warm or friendly relationship, Edward Seaga held Mayer Matalon in high regard. His open support of the PNP notwithstanding, Seaga recognized that Mayer was a nationalist not a partisan, and that he had valuable insight into a range of issues affecting national development. Furthermore, ICD and WIHCON were too large and too important to the Jamaican economy for the Matalons' support of the PNP to be a barrier to a JLP government working with them.

Dhiru Tanna, an economist and businessman who made his home in Jamaica in 1973 after the Ugandan Asian expulsion by Idi Amin, made the introduction. Tanna had met Mayer when he was an adviser in the Ministry of Public Utilities. As chairman of the Jamaica Telephone Company (JTC), the state-owned telecommunications services provider, Mayer had to apply for rate increases through Tanna; they became friends. Disenchanted with the

PNP's turn to the Left and cognizant of its deleterious effect on the economy, Tanna helped the JLP with its manifesto, and after the JLP victory, had the prime minister's ear with regard to board appointments. He knew that Mayer still wanted to contribute politically, regardless of his relationship with Michael Manley and the PNP, and that his knowledge, expertise and his international financial contacts could be a valuable resource to the government. Seaga reappointed Mayer Matalon to chair the Jamaica Telephone Company board, and appointed him a director (later chairman) of the National Investment Bank of Jamaica. These were two important entities for Seaga's plans to modernize and expand the Jamaican economy. Board directorships and chairmanships were reserved for party insiders and favorites and appointing Mayer to these positions was indicative of the trust that Seaga had in him. (It was during his tenure as chairman of Jamaica Telephone Company, later Telecommunications of Jamaica, that the telecommunications industry in Jamaica was transformed, a topic elaborated on in a separate chapter.)

The association with Seaga had its low points. One of the hallmarks of Seaga's plans for Jamaica was a modernization and overhaul of Jamaican agriculture under the investment program AGRO 21. AGRO 21 was intended as the panacea for all Jamaica's developmental ills: it would increase domestic food production, expand export production, provide employment and skills training, and earn foreign exchange.[22]

Through AGRO 21 Seaga wanted to produce a showcase project that would symbolize Jamaica's modern agricultural potential. That project was Spring Plains, a joint venture between the Jamaica National Investment Corporation (National Investment Bank of Jamaica, NIBJ) and an Israeli businessman, Eli Tisona. The company and vehicle for the project was Jamaica Agro Products (JAP), and Mayer, who was chairman of the NIBJ, was also made chairman of JAP.[23]

Shortly after the project had been announced and had started operations—growing vegetables in Clarendon for the North American market and transporting them by plane directly to the United States—rumors began to circulate in Jamaica that Tisona had a criminal past in Israel. Seaga asked Mayer to go to Israel to investigate the allegations; Mayer did so, and found them to be baseless. He went on national television to defend Seaga and the project, a task that he reluctantly felt obliged to fulfill despite his loathing of such dramatic publicity. His son Joseph later said it was probably one of the most unpleasant assignments he ever had to carry out.

That did not stop the accusations that Spring Plains was a front for money laundering and drug trafficking, aspersions that dogged Seaga and Mayer for years. The project foundered and was put into receivership after just three years, having lost millions of US dollars and with little prospect of ever succeeding. The impact of the Spring Plains failure, and the surrounding allegations and controversy, had a marked negative effect on Seaga and the JLP's image in the Jamaican political imagination, and undoubtedly was a significant factor in the subsequent drop in popular support for the administration. The bad taste left by the Spring Plains debacle contributed to the ensuing decline in the JLP's electoral prospects, culminating in the JLP's loss in the 1989 elections. Eli Tisona, who was later described by the *New York Times* as a "Miami crime boss," was convicted in Florida in 1999 for his role as an investment counselor to and money launderer for Colombia's Cali cartel.[24]

When Michael Manley was reelected in 1989, Mayer Matalon was one of his key advisors, officially and unofficially. He was appointed to Michael's personal committee of "five wise men,"[25] officially called the Economic Advisory Council, along with G. Arthur Brown, Barclay Ewart, Owen Jefferson and Omar Davies. He regularly travelled with the prime minister on official missions and maintained ongoing dialogue with him on virtually every matter of state policy and decision making. Through his personal contacts, Mayer Matalon arranged for the US president, George Bush, to invite Manley to the White House. Even with the renewed political and personal relationship between them, Michael did not always accept Mayer's advice, most pointedly when he recommended against foreign exchange liberalization in 1991.

The only Jamaican leader that Mayer Matalon did not work closely with was P. J. Patterson. They had known each other since Patterson was a young man working with Norman Manley in the 1950s. They first met when Mayer was in London as part of Norman Manley's entourage for discussions about the Federation and, later independence; Patterson was a law student there. On Patterson's return to Jamaica, he interacted with Mayer (and many of the Matalon brothers) as Michael Manley's campaign manager in his bid for the PNP party leadership in 1969, as the PNP prepared for the 1972 elections, and during the subsequent PNP administration, given the overlap of their respective roles in the party and the government. Where Mayer was an advisor to the government in many different areas, Patterson occupied different cabinet portfolios, including finance and planning. Their relationship was very cordial, in keeping with Mayer's valued support for the PNP.

The relationship shifted with what came to be known as the "Shell Waiver Scandal." Shell Oil, the oil and gas multinational, had operated in Jamaica since the 1920s. In 1989, when the PNP assumed office, Shell Oil's operations chief was a member of the PNP's National Executive Committee (the party's highest governing body). In 1991 it came to light that, in his capacity as minister of finance, Patterson had waived millions of dollars in duties for Shell's importation of unleaded gasoline. There are contesting accounts as to whether or not the waiver was corruption, as the media frenzy then purported, or a misunderstanding of the complicated duty regime that existed at the time. A 2016 authorized biography of Michael Manley claimed that Patterson had acted in good faith,[26] but Patterson's own memoir tells a slightly more complicated story.

Eli Matalon, Mayer's brother, was chairman of the Petroleum Corporation of Jamaica and resigned in protest on the granting of the waiver; he went on to publicly and vociferously impugn Patterson. While Manley didn't directly ask for Patterson's resignation (that is, fire him), the cabinet was reshuffled and Patterson excluded from the new grouping. Patterson was sideswiped. The move was considered extreme in the circumstances and in the context of Jamaica's political norms and customs. In his memoir Patterson describes this period as "by far the most hurtful and agonizing in my life."[27]

The question as to why did Manley treat Patterson as he did is key to what would come to be the relationship between Mayer Matalon and P. J. Patterson thereafter. An explanation that was held to by Patterson's supporters within the PNP was that the Shell issue was a red herring that conveniently masked what was really happening in the party. In Howard Hamilton's own words, "Powerful influences convinced the ailing Michael Manley that this was an excellent opportunity to get rid of his deputy [and] not allow the legacy of his father, Norman Manley, to pass to Patterson and his black mafia."[28] (Hamilton was the Shell operations chief, and one of Patterson's close political allies.) These "powerful influences," according to that view, undoubtedly included Mayer and Eli Matalon, who were then, as before, Michael's close confidantes; the "palace guard," as it were, "seeking to stoke fire."[29] Whatever the real story with regard to the waiver and Patterson's removal from his position as minister and deputy prime minister, the episode cast the Matalons as the villains, and the personification of the "big man" from the "old order" throwing his weight around.

When he became prime minister in March 1992, two months after his removal from the cabinet, these wounds were still fresh, and in any event were unlikely to be healed, as Patterson had his own team of advisors and confidantes, of influencers and power brokers, with their own ideas about the distribution of power in Jamaica and transitioning from the previous social and economic order. Patterson distanced himself from Michael Manley and in so doing he also distanced himself from the people Michael was close to, regardless of the role they had played in previous administrations, or the expertise and connections they possessed. In Patterson's own kitchen cabinet, one of the most powerful people was Vin Lawrence—himself a brilliant man and fine negotiator—who many in the PNP jokingly called "the black Matalon."[30] For his part, Mayer lamented, "He is the only Prime Minister who I can't pick up the phone and call."[31] It was a discomfiting loss of influence and a blow to his ego. This break between Mayer and his access to power ended up being far more significant than Mayer's ego being bruised, however. Though it does not become clear until years later, the souring of the relationship with Patterson, and Mayer's exclusion from having Patterson's ear, would have severe ramifications for Mayer, his family, his family's business, and for Jamaica.

Mayer's legacy as counselor to the powers that be was not entirely scuttled during the Patterson administration. Omar Davies, Patterson's minister of finance, relied on Mayer, as did his financial secretary, Shirley Tyndall, who considered him her mentor. They were in constant dialogue, as she sought his advice on a wide range of matters, and depended on his contacts to finance the government in various ways, especially through transactions with the Bank of Nova Scotia. But access to them was not enough for Mayer's advice to be heeded when it really mattered. Davies and Tyndall both recall Mayer foreseeing the financial crisis of the late 1990s and his recommendations that the necessary corrections could be made without a major financial cost.[32] This is not a benign recollection.

From Mayer's vantage point at BNS it was clear to him that all was not well in the Jamaican financial system. As early as 1993 he had warned the relevant people in the Ministry of Finance of impending problems. Mayer had then been asked by Davies to look more closely at the situation with the banks and to advise him; to this extent Mayer was given access to inspection reports done by the Bank of Jamaica. He was shocked by what he saw. A number of the new "indigenous" banks that had been established in the early 1990s were woefully undercapitalized, were extending unrealistic interest rates to get funds, and had large amounts of bad debts. Banking regulations were being sidestepped by the formation of poorly regulated "building societies." Mayer's recommendations were to immediately regularize the banks by way of closures, mergers and acquisitions.

Mayer's advice was ignored, but not just because he was exiled from the inner sanctum of political and decision-making power. The banks themselves were powerful political symbols and closing them was not considered, by the powers that were, an option. The government was "committed to broadening Jamaican ownership in the [banking] sector."[33] Beyond their functional aspects, banks, and who controls them, are important symbols of economic power and economic nationalism. The Jamaican-owned banks and financial institutions that had emerged in the early 1990s were potent symbols of the rising black Jamaican entrepreneurial class whose time had finally come.[34] The sale of Workers Bank is emblematic of the dynamics then at play. Workers Bank had been founded in 1973 during the early days of Jamaica's attempts at economic nationalism with the express purpose of financing local development. In 1991 it was privatized and sold to a group of black Jamaican entrepreneurs with little banking experience; their bid won out over bids by people who were much more experienced in the financial sector but who were also from what would have then been considered the traditional privileged class. Workers Bank and the other new indigenous banks were held up by the government and the media as nationalistic examples of the rise and success of the ordinary Jamaican. Aside from banking services, many of the indigenous banks invested widely in tourism, agriculture and real estate, which was encouraged by official government policy support for the expansion of the domestic financial sector into the productive sector, again with an economic nationalistic objective.

The official investigations in the aftermath of the subsequent financial collapse bore out Mayer's findings and predictions. It was discovered that many of the banks had unreliable financial statements, inaccurate Bank of Jamaica reporting, nonexistent investments recorded on their books, bank loans diverted to subsidiary companies to avoid reporting as past due, misstating financial statements and inflating balances, among other discrepancies.

Davies and Tyndall, twenty-plus years later, readily proffer that Mayer's recommendations, had they been adopted, would have protected small depositors, who were the majority of the banks' customers, at a cost that was a fraction of the cost of what ultimately happened, with the wholesale bailout of the financial sector, the collapse of hundreds of businesses, and the huge debt accumulation that financed the bailout.[35] And, as it would turn out, with far fewer deleterious effects on ICD, and its attempts to recover from the same crisis.

In a speech some years later, in reference to the lead up to the financial sector collapse, Omar Davies admitted to what he called "errors," in that he had "indulged in some amount of social engineering by encouraging indigenous participation in the ownership and control of major banking institutions . . . [and] that in his zealousness to achieve a sociological objective he stepped over the line in giving 'blighs' (unmerited favors) to individuals who would be proved by later developments to be either unworthy of such considerations or incapable of making good on them."[36]

The issues of the banks in the early 1990s were not, as Davies's comments make clear, merely economic, and taking remedial action at the time was not just a matter of prudent policy. These banks, and what they represented, were politically important, and deeply so, as they represented a triumph over the old order with their ostensible creation of a black Jamaican wealthy class. Coupled with his extant exile from the inner circle, on this matter in particular, Mayer's advice was certainly not going to be heeded.

Mayer's last engagement as financial guru and advisor was with Bruce Golding, Jamaica's prime minister from 2007–2011. Hugh Shearer had introduced them in the late 1970s. Golding was minister of housing in the JLP government in the 1980s and they interacted regularly. By coincidence they were both in London when Hurricane Gilbert devastated Jamaica in September 1988. Through Mayer's contacts with Cable and Wireless they were able to find out what was happening, and keep in touch. Mayer supported Golding when he left the JLP and formed the National Democratic Movement in 1996, including donating to the fledgling third party, though it only lasted a few years and Golding eventually returned to the JLP. Golding continued to seek Mayer's counsel throughout his tenure as prime minister, and to rely on him to broker deals between the Bank of Nova Scotia and the government, though Mayer was not as directly involved in the government as he had been in decades past. Golding's respect for him and the strength of their relationship was demonstrated when he visited him two weeks before he died.

Every prime minister, and indeed every minister, has their advisors and confidantes. Senior-level decision makers, especially in the areas of finance and the economy, have to maintain dialogue with the private sector via individuals whom they trust, and with the people and companies occupying the commanding heights of the economy. In that regard, the fact that Mayer Matalon advised or played a role as a businessman in politics or government is unremarkable. What is extraordinary, however, is that he advised and played an important role over such a long period of time, across political parties, and for so many leaders. There is no other single person in Jamaica who has had the influence and connections to power of Mayer Matalon, or who was so instrumental in so many significant policy decisions, over such a long period of time. In this regard he was unique. It is unlikely that we will ever again see anyone like Mayer Matalon in Jamaican political life.

NOTES

1. "Business: Another Matalon Milestone," *Newday* 7, no. 3 (March, 1963).
2. Mayer Matalon, "The Management of Change," speech delivered at luncheon of the Jamaican-American Chamber of Commerce, May 18, 1976 (Kingston: Agency for Public Information, 1976).
3. Colin A. Palmer, *Freedom's Children: The 1938 Labour Rebellion and the Birth of Modern Jamaica* (Kingston: Ian Randle Publishers, 2014).
4. "House approves Hughenden housing scheme," *Gleaner*, August 18, 1967, 17.
5. Interview with an acquaintance of Mayer Matalon, June 2018. This story has been repeated elsewhere.
6. Matalon, "Growing up in Kingston."
7. Interview with a Matalon family member, June 9, 2017.
8. Ibid.

9. Interview with an acquaintance of Mayer Matalon, June 15, 2015.

10. Hugh Lawson Shearer, "New Year's Message," January 1, 1970, www.rjrnewsonline.com/archive/new-years-message-1970-prime-minister-hugh-lawson-shearer.

11. Carlton E. Davis, *Jamaica in the World Aluminium Industry Volume II–Bauxite Levy Negotiations, 1974–1988* (Kingston: Jamaica Bauxite Institute, 1989).

12. Alvin G. Wint, "Has the Obsolescing Bargain Obsolesced? Negotiating with Foreign Investors," in *International Business and Government Relations in the 21st Century*, ed. Robert Grosse (Cambridge: Cambridge University Press, 2011), 315–38.

13. "Jamaican Leader Seeking Minimum Price for Bauxite," *New York Times*, June 4, 1975. www.nytimes.com/1975/06/04/archives/jamaican-leader-seeking-minimum-price-for-bauxite.html

14. Joseph B. Treaster, "Jamaica, Close U.S. Ally, Does Little to Halt Drugs," *New York Times*, September 10, 1984, www.nytimes.com/1984/09/10/world/jamaica-close-us-ally-does-little-to-halt-drugs.html?pagewanted=all.

15. US Embassy, Kingston, Telegram 253 to the Department of State, Washington DC, January 19, 1976, www.history.state.gov/historicaldocuments/frus1969-76ve11p1/d459.

16. Matalon, "The Management of Change."

17. Matalon family member interview, ibid.

18. Darrell E. Levi, *Michael Manley: The Making of a Leader* (Kingston: Heinemann Caribbean, 1989), 132.

19. Elaine Ferguson, "The Matalons," *Money Index* 324, no. 16 (June 1992): 19.

20. Matalon family member interview, ibid.

21. Manley, *In My Father's Shade*.

22. Bryan, *Edward Seaga*, 240–41.

23. Edward Seaga, *My Life and Leadership Volume II: Hard Road to Travel 1980–2008* (Oxford: Macmillan, 2010), 72.

24. William A. Orme, "Israel Seen as a Paradise for Money Laundering," *New York Times*, February 21, 2000, www.nytimes.com/2000/02/21/world/israel-seen-as-paradise-for-money-laundering.html.

25. Matalon acquaintance interview, 2015, ibid.

26. Godfrey Smith, *Michael Manley: The Biography* (Kingston: Ian Randle Publishers, 2016).

27. P. J. Patterson, *My Political Journey: Jamaica's Sixth Prime Minister* (Kingston: University of the West Indies Press, 2018), 198.

28. Howard Hamilton, "Petroleum Industry in Chaos," *Gleaner*, November 27, 2016, www.jamaica-gleaner.com/article/focus/20161127/howard-hamilton-petroleum-industry-chaos.

29. Patterson, *My Political Journey*, 162.

30. Two PNP insiders, in separate interviews, shared this anecdote with me. In Patterson's memoir, Vin Lawrence heads the list of his team at the Office of the Prime Minister when he assumed office.

31. Interview with acquaintance of Mayer Matalon, January 19, 2016.

32. Shirley Tyndall, personal interview, October 23, 2016; Omar Davies, personal interview, June 25, 2015.

33. Patterson, *My Political Journey*, 161.

34. Diana Thorburn, "Nationalism, Identity and the Banking Sector: The English-speaking Caribbean in the Era of Financial Globalization," in *Ethnicity, Race and Nationalism in the Caribbean*, ed. Anton Allahar (New York: Lexington Press, 2005), 57–84.

35. Tyndall, ibid; Davies, ibid.

36. Henley Morgan, "Dr. Davies' Mea Culpa," *Observer*, October 25, 2002.

Chapter Eight

Jamaica's Chairman of the Board: Bank of Nova Scotia and Cable and Wireless

Chairman *extraordinaire* was a role that came naturally to Mayer Matalon.[1] His tenure as a director of the Bank of Nova Scotia (Jamaica) from 1966 until 2011, the year before he died, encompassed more than the contribution of a financial wizard and Jamaican business insider to one of Jamaica's most important financial entities. In his forty-five years there, Mayer not only led the Jamaican operation to being one of its Canadian parent company's most profitable subsidiaries, among some fifty overseas entities, but he also played a crucial role as intermediary between the government of Jamaica and the bank as a financier of Jamaican government debt and cash flow.

Scotia Bank, or BNS, had been in Jamaica since 1889, originally as a financier of trade between the colonies and North America. They held the Jamaican government's accounts from 1906 onwards, successfully capturing them from the Colonial Bank (UK). Depending on who is measuring, it is the most profitable bank and one of the most profitable companies in Jamaica.

Mayer Matalon joined the board of the Bank of Nova Scotia (Jamaica) in 1966. At the age of forty-four Mayer was already considered a brilliant entrepreneur, from a leading business family, with a conglomerate of companies involved in many different areas of the economy. BNS had been banker to the Matalon family's businesses. Mayer's talent and expertise were by now well known in Jamaica and beyond, and his invitation to join BNS was a shrewd move on BNS's part.

The significant initiative that BNS made shortly thereafter, of inviting more Jamaicans onto the board and offering shares to the public, was put to the bank by Mayer. He felt that, as large an institution as BNS was in the Jamaican landscape, it should have more Jamaican participation on its executive, and should encourage Jamaican ownership through a public share offering. Recognizing the shifting political and social climate of the time, the Canadian parent company, in 1967, reconstituted the bank as a publicly traded company, offering 25 percent of its shares to Jamaicans. (In 1970 it moved to 30 percent.) The board of directors was reconfigured to include four Jamaicans, prominent businessmen from different parts of the island.

For most of Mayer's tenure at BNS he was deputy chairman, but considered by most to be the *de facto* chairman. The chairman always had to be someone from the Canada head office, but they generally travelled infrequently to Jamaica and Mayer more often than not chaired board meetings and was entrusted with making decisions and taking actions that normally would have been the chairman's purview.

His contribution to the bank, which he served as if it were his own business, is legendary. He was able to marry his insight into the Jamaican economy and business environment, with his relationships with government and political actors, and his knowledge of the world of finance, including global finance, to the bank's benefit. The bank enjoyed decades of unbroken profitability, even during Jamaica's most difficult economic downturns in the 1970s and the late 1990s, no doubt guided by Mayer's intimate knowledge and understanding of the Jamaican economy and the government policies that affected it. In return, the bank has honored him in various ways, including establishing a scholarship in his name in 2006, tenable in the Department of Management Studies at the University of the West Indies, Mona.

Mayer Matalon was also able to broker many delicate transactions, some at very short notice, between the Jamaican government and the bank, rescuing the government from serious fallout and even collapse. His personal relationships with so many of the different players in the government and in Canada were immensely helpful, as they allowed for a trust in him that gave him the leverage to make bold proposals and hold hard lines in a negotiation. In his tribute to Mayer Matalon at his memorial service in 2012, Omar Davies publicly recounted the details of one such occasion, where he saved the administration by arranging a special loan at very short notice, providing the government with the money to make its pay bill on the Friday before Christmas.[2]

Mayer was involved in the micro aspects of the bank's operations, forming close relationships with the managers, including mentoring employees as they moved up the ladder of seniority in the institution. Many employees went through what they called his "negotiation school." He would personally guide them on strategy and tactics ahead of important negotiations, and be on call—available by phone during breaks to give guidance in the actual negotiation—for consultations as to whether things were going as expected, and how to proceed.[3]

One of his mentees, one might even call him his protégée, was Bill Clarke, BNS CEO of thirteen years. They spoke every day, often many times a day, for over a decade, as together they directed and conducted the bank's business. In 1998 Clarke said in an interview, "He is, to me, one of the best human beings with whom I have interacted. He is genuine to the core and never afraid to speak his mind."[4]

One of Mayer's last major actions at BNS was his attempt to mediate between BNS and Clarke, in 2008–2009. Amid allegations of misconduct, Clarke was unwillingly separated from the bank. In the early stages of what turned into a five-year legal battle between Clarke and the bank, Mayer, going against the opinions of many of the other board members, defended Clarke and advocated on his behalf with Canada. Though Mayer was seeking to secure a generous settlement, more favorable to Clarke than many on the Jamaican board or in Canada thought he deserved, Clarke thought that Mayer was working against him. Clarke rejected the settlement offer and scuttled his decades-long relationship with Mayer.

BNS also did business with ICD and the Matalon family, mainly through Mayer. In 1988 the bank and ICD embarked on a joint venture, creating Industrial Finance Holdings Limited, a holding company comprising Industrial Finance Corporation, International Insurance Brokers Limited, and British Caribbean Insurance Company. This was BNS's entrée into the Jamaican financial services market, beyond banking. (They later sold their half to Mechala, the holding company that acquired ICD's subsidiaries, in 1996.) When the Mechala bond offering went awry, BNS provided the US$20 million loan to Mayer, which helped to buy out the bondholders.

Mayer Matalon was, and always will be, a unique figure in his role at BNS—unique to BNS broadly speaking and unique to Jamaica. He acted as a bridge between a multinational financial institution and a developing country government, in a way that was unprecedented and probably never to be replicated, particularly given modern day bank regulation and governance policies.

His leadership of the Jamaica Telephone Company (JTC) through its transition to Telecommunications of Jamaica (TOJ) (fig 8.1) and eventually Cable and Wireless (C&W) Jamaica, was also exceptional in the landmark nature of the developments that occurred during his stewardship, and their importance to Jamaica's development.

Telecommunications is today, as it has been at least since the 1980s, a critical component of a country's economy and participation in the world. Mayer Matalon played a significant role in the development of Jamaica's telecommunications sector. He was a director of the Jamaica Telephone Company (JTC) from 1961 and became its chairman in 1972. He stayed on as chairman in 1980, presided over the privatization of Jamaica's telecommunications in the late 1980s, and was in a position of leadership and influence in the lead-up to the liberalization of Jamaica's telecoms sector in 1999.

Figure 8.1. Mayer Matalon, in his capacity as chairman, carrying out the ceremonial listing of Telecommunications of Jamaica (TOJ) on the Jamaica Stock Exchange, October 27, 1988
Courtesy of the Gleaner Company (Media) Limited

As an important outpost of the British colonial empire, Jamaica and the rest of the English-speaking Caribbean, have had, since the advent of telecommunications, relatively modern systems. From the mid-1800s to the 1990s, the Jamaican telecommunications sector was dominated by the British telecoms giant, Cable and Wireless, whether as a supplier of technology and service to a government-owned entity, or as majority shareholder in a divested, private telecommunications company.

The company initially operated as a service provider to the British colonial government. After independence in 1962, the Jamaican government, as was the trend among newly independent countries, took a majority shareholding in what was then called the Jamaica Telephone Company. With a majority shareholding the government could regulate policy and dictate employment, services and rates. Jamintel, the company governing and operating connections between Jamaica and the rest of the world, was 49 percent owned by Cable and Wireless UK, which provided the technology and service.

The 1970s was the beginning of dramatic technological changes in telecommunications, accompanied by significant increases in the scale of investment needed to keep up with them, as well as a greater need for technical know-how and management sophistication. Government-owned and run telecommunications entities, particularly in developing countries and specifically in Jamaica, which experienced an economic contraction, lacked the capacity to keep pace with technological developments and deliver modern telecommunications services to the public. In Jamaica this was manifest in a years-long waiting list to get a home phone (what came to be called a "landline"). For a few years, in a desperate effort to appease the unmet demand, "party lines" were offered where different households shared a line, though they had individual phone numbers. If one wanted to make a call and the other party was on the phone, they had to wait until the line was free. The general public was highly aware of the deficiencies of the service.

Then came the 1980s and Jamaica's attempts at recovery from a decade of economic volatility and high levels of indebtedness, in the context of a global trend of developing countries privatizing their utilities to reduce the size of their governments. These conditions augured well for the privatization of the island's telecommunications.

In 1988, Cable and Wireless UK reacquired a majority share, 79 percent, in what then became Telecommunications of Jamaica (TOJ), a consolidation of JTC and Jamintel. C&W UK via TOJ also acquired a set of exclusive government licenses to be the sole provider of telecommunications services in Jamaica for the next twenty-five years and beyond. During this period Jamaican telecommunications were vastly improved as the company expanded its offerings and updated its technology, including providing internet service, bringing Jamaica closer to world standards, with all the attendant benefits to multiple other sectors in the economy and society.

On this platform, and through Mayer Matalon's initiative, Jamaica's modern business processing outsourcing (BPO) industry was established and inaugurated in 1988. The first "Digiport," in the Montego Bay freezone, was a partnership between the Government of Jamaica (GoJ), C&W and US telecoms giant AT&T. By 2016 BPO was one of Jamaica's most important and fastest growing sectors, comprising forty companies and employing fourteen thousand people.[5]

The twenty-five-year licenses issued in 1988 ensured TOJ a monopoly over all aspects of the island's wired telephone network, a term that was considered by many experts to be unduly generous, compared with the global industry standard of seven to ten years. Another aspect of the agreement that was a cause of concern was the rate of return guaranteed to C&W, including granting the company the right to raise rates as necessary.[6] Both of these were the subjects of extensive and ongoing debates across Jamaica, aided particularly by the increasing spread of radio call-in programs.

Mayer Matalon unapologetically defended the agreement, arguing that in a small country like Jamaica only a monopoly could be viable, and that without a guaranteed return no company would make the investments necessary to bring Jamaica's telecommunications technology up to scratch. Having chaired the Jamaica Telephone Company when it was fully government-owned, he had the measure of what a properly-run telecommunications system cost. The rates charged by JTC were too low for capital to be invested to improve and maintain the technology and service. In the 1970s, he would apply to the Ministry of Public Utilities for a rate increase to improve services and infrastructure, as did all other government-owned public utilities. The application would then go to court. It would take years to get a hearing and then another year to get a decision, during which time inflation would render the applied-for rate increase irrelevant, and the technology by then obsolete. The service remained inadequate, poor and outdated. It was not an argument that the average Jamaican consumer understood well; people wanted modern telephone and communication services but did not grasp the real cost. Most Jamaicans also could not comprehend that in a developing country with virtually no infrastructure, in the global telecommunications industry context, at the time, a monopoly was the only way to build out a modern network, a point which sensationalizing radio talk-show hosts would fail to explain, preferring instead to go for the knee-jerk negative reaction to the general concept of a monopoly.

Mayer was the lead negotiator for the government in the sale of its shares to C&W, which took the entity fully private. After the sale was finalized, he was reappointed by C&W to chair the now private entity, a position he held through further transitions to the entity's shareholdings and branding, until 1998. During this time Mayer worked closely with C&W UK's chairman Lord David Young. Lord Young was the former minister of trade and industry (unelected) in Margaret Thatcher's cabinet and was considered a powerful figure in the United Kingdom and internationally. He and Mayer became fast friends and got along very well. Like Sir Brian Mountain, Lord Young was impressed with and charmed by Mayer's genius and vision.

Throughout those years, C&W Jamaica was extraordinarily profitable. At one point the company accounted for almost three quarters of the market capitalization of the Jamaica Stock Exchange. Outside of C&W's Jamaican operation Mayer Matalon negotiated the parent company's takeover of the Panamanian telecommunications system, and was appointed a director on the board of Cable and Wireless Panama. In the early nineties Mayer facilitated the engagement of newly-retired prime minister, Michael Manley, as a paid consultant to Cable and Wireless UK, when they sought to buy Cuba's telephone company, so they could broker Manley's ties to Cuba and his relationship with Fidel Castro.[7] (The deal was ultimately unsuccessful.)

Prior to the end of his tenure at Cable and Wireless, Mayer Matalon had advised the parent company, in light of the impending entry of Digicel and others into the wireless communications market, to engage in another massive capital expenditure to upgrade the quality of its mobile network. However, Mayer's relationship with C&W UK had shifted after Lord Young stepped down from the position of executive chairman in late 1996. Dick Brown, the American executive who took over from Lord Young, was a tiger of an altogether different stripe. Brash, outspoken and charismatic, he came into the position with a completely different vision for C&W and of corporate governance. Lord Young and Mayer Matalon were of the era of the imperial chairman, where they were able to make and take decisions among themselves. Brown, however, had little regard for what he considered ascribed status and the old way of doing things. Brown, shortly after assuming the position at C&W, kept Mayer waiting for over half an hour to see him, an affront which presaged the souring of the relationship between Mayer and C&W UK. Brown saw Mayer's main role as maintaining the company's relationship with the government and protecting the license, and tolerated him because the license was key to C&W's continued success in their Jamaican business.

Dick Brown undertook a massive redirection of C&W's interests, doing a 180-degree turn from Young's global expansionist agenda. He invested heavily in data and internet, and sold off stakes in a number of mobile telephone interests around the world.[8] At the same time, the Jamaican election of 1997 returned the PNP to office, but cabinet portfolios were reassigned. Robert "Bobby" Pickersgill, who was minister of public utilities and transport, was effectively replaced by Phillip Paulwell, who was assigned to a newly-created Ministry of Commerce and Technology with responsibility for telecoms. Paulwell was considered to be "pro-liberalizing" and styled himself as a forward-thinking mover and shaker. On assuming office he made clear his intentions to realize the potential for development of the information technology sector in its own right, and as a component of a developmentalist national industrial policy. In addition, Jamaica, against Mayer Matalon's advice, had signed on to the World Trade Organization (WTO) Agreement on Telecommunications, which in principle provided for competition in wireless and network services. In this context, with the license threatened by the changed political dynamics in Jamaica, and with the relationship between Brown and Matalon being so markedly different from what it had been during Lord Young's tenure, C&W UK did not support Mayer's entrepreneurial vision for the company's operations in Jamaica.

Together with Errald Miller, C&W Jamaica's widely respected president since 1995, they had long arguments with the parent company executives on the board. C&W UK could not foresee that a poor country like Jamaica would have such a large appetite for expensive mobile services, and did not think the return on investment would be worthwhile. The head office did not comprehend the scale, scope and potential of the Jamaican mobile telecommunications market, nor the sophistication of the Jamaican consumer, and underestimated the threat of the new competition. Mayer and Miller understood this, but were unable to convince the decision makers in London. Up to that point, the company had drastically underestimated the Jamaican market for mobile services and had oversold its service far beyond its capacity. It had gained a terrible reputation among Jamaican mobile services consumers for providing shoddy service at a high cost, and many customers abandoned them for their competitors as soon as they—namely Digicel, an Irish company—made landfall. Nor, apparently, did C&W UK believe that the Jamaican government was sophisticated enough to go through with the liberalization of the industry and perhaps held out that it wouldn't actually happen.

It was a great disappointment to Mayer that they did not follow his advice or trust his foresight. He did not wield the influence he once had, not with the company or with the government, and that was difficult for him to come to terms with. In 1999, shortly after he stepped down from the C&W chairmanship, the Jamaican government ended the agreement with C&W, bought out the licenses, and embarked on a phased liberalization of the telecommunications sector. Cable and Wireless's monopoly ended and the Jamaican communications marketplace was redefined.

C&W UK suffered its own demise when the dot-com bubble burst in 2000.[9] The company was forced into a massive restructuring, lost its place on the Financial Times Stock Exchange 100 Index (a share index of the one hundred companies listed on the London Stock Exchange with the highest market capitalization), and experienced a catastrophic destruction of shareholder value.[10] In tandem, though of a completely different genesis, C&W Jamaica went from one of the most profitable companies on the island into a downward spiral from which it only recovered, after numerous restructuring efforts and enormous debt write-offs, over fifteen years later.

Mayer Matalon brought Jamaican telecommunications from party lines to having one of the highest telecommunications penetration per capita in the world, and one of the most modern communications systems in the hemisphere. Defending the monopoly was an unpopular position, and perhaps Mayer sought to maintain the monopoly beyond its usefulness and relevance, but the initial build out of Jamaica's telecommunications infrastructure under the monopoly arrangement with Cable and Wireless laid the foundation for the country's ability to rapidly absorb new communications technologies as they were developed in the decades thereafter.

NOTES

1. Gordon Robinson, "Mayer Matalon—Jamaica's 'Chairman of the Board,'" *Gleaner*, 22 July 2012.

2. Davies, "Eulogy."

3. Michael D. Jones, personal email to Joseph M. Matalon, 6 February 2012.

4. Barbara Ellington, "William 'Bill' Clarke, 40 Years at the Number One Bank," *Gleaner*, May 18, 2000, 36.

5. "Business Process Outsourcing Carrying the Swing: Let's Go for It!" *Observer*, January 12, 2016, www.jamaicaobserver.com/editorial/Business-Process-Outsourcing-carrying-the-swing--Let-s-go-for-it-_48498.

6. Hopeton Dunn and Winston Gooden, "Telecommunications Policy Making in Jamaica: From State Monopoly to Private Monopoly," in *Telecommunications in Latin America*, ed. Eli Noam (Oxford: Oxford University Press, 1997), 73–81.

7. Smith, *Michael Manley*.

8. "How a Globe-Girdling Enterprise Snapped," *Daily Telegraph*, February 1, 2006. www.telegraph.co.uk/finance/2931252/How-a-globe-girdling-enterprise-snapped.html.

9. Richard Wray, "Ten Years after the Crash, the Dotcom Boom Can Finally Come of Age," *Guardian*, March 14, 2010, www.theguardian.com/business/2010/mar/14/technology-dotcom-crash-2000.

10. Richard Wray and Jill Treanor, "High Price of C&W Salvation," *Guardian*, January 11, 2003. www.theguardian.com/business/2003/jan/11/4.

Chapter Nine

The End of an Era

By 1994 the Matalon family—the surviving siblings and those of their children who were shareholders—came to the agreement that the businesses, and the debt, had to be restructured and refinanced. This was not a new discussion; they had known that they needed to reduce their indebtedness since at least the mid-1980s, and had discussed strategies, but no action had been taken given the divergence in views, primarily between Mayer and his son Joe M., and most of the rest of the family. Some of the third generation Matalons who were either working in the business and shareholders (or both), had their own opinions and approaches. Disputes and grievances arose as a result and translated to bitterness between the siblings, who sought to protect their own children's interests. Conflicting views on how to proceed were further complicated by the extant tensions that originated with the mass move to Miami in the 1970s.

While the liberalization of the foreign exchange market in the early 1990s (against which Mayer had warned Manley) had some benefits for ICD's subsidiaries by relieving the foreign exchange shortage, any gains were undone by continually rising interest rates. For a company as highly leveraged as ICD and its subsidiaries, this meant interest rates outpaced income and profit margins—that is, the debt increased while profits decreased. In 1994, the Matalons reported net losses of US$5.3 million.

Mayer proposed, and the family eventually agreed, that publicly held ICD shares should be bought back by the family and a new company formed. Mechala Investments became the umbrella for all the former ICD subsidiaries and WIHCON. Some of the businesses owned and operated by the Matalons had already been closed or sold—Caribbean Brush Company, the 807 hosiery factory, the paint manufacturing operation, and Homelectrix—either because they were no longer viable or to raise much-needed cash. United Motors, for example, though an extremely profitable company that was set to become even more so with the liberalization of the car market, was sold in 1980 to raise cash for those who had migrated but continued to rely on the Jamaica businesses for income. WIHCON, which had always been privately held by the Matalon family, was now incorporated as a subsidiary with the other businesses, which were then reorganized into a Development and Construction Division, a Manufacturing and Trading Division, and a Financial Services Division.

The restructuring was initially conceptualized by Mayer and his son, Joseph M., with Mayer as chairman and Joseph M. as Chief Operating Officer. With the incorporation of WIHCON into the new entity, WIHCON's managing director—Aaron's son, Joseph A.—was named president. Aside from the very real work they put into the initiative, Joe A. and Joe M. were, quite literally, the poster boys for Mechala. The iconic image of the two handsome scions of the Matalon family that came to represent the Mechala endeavor conveyed the neat impression that this was a handing down of the family business to the next generation. It was considerably more complex than that.

There was one priority: to reduce the debt. To access cheaper debt the Matalons had to look outside Jamaica; accordingly they went to the United States, where they sought to introduce an initial public offering (IPO) to raise money. It was a bold idea, in keeping with the Matalons' legacy of innovation and large-scale thinking. They would have been the first Jamaican company to list on the US stock market. This was the modern day equivalent of Mayer going to Eagle Star to get financing for their first housing development.

The North American firm, Merrill Lynch, was engaged to facilitate a US$100 million equity offering on the New York Stock Exchange or the Nasdaq. Due diligence and all the extensive paperwork for this had been completed, and the issuance was to be done in December 1996. In November 1996, based on market conditions, Merrill Lynch advised that they convert it to a short-term debt offering, with a view to refinancing it through an equity offering after three years.

When the IPO plan was shelved, as they thought temporarily, the Matalons moved to a bond issue, with the intention of pursuing the IPO later. The costs, logistics, time and effort that went into this endeavor were immense. Mechala had engaged the most reputable financial and legal firms in the United States to do the work, as well as a phalanx of personnel in Jamaica. To proceed with the bond issue, they had to harmonize Jamaican and US accounting standards and meet multiple legal and financial reporting requirements. At the same time, they were modernizing the human resources and business processes in the Mechala subsidiaries so as to revamp management and operations toward more sustainable and better profitability.

The bond issue, also a first for a Jamaican company in the United States, went ahead in 1996 and raised US$100 million, a good portion of which went to pay off J$2.8 billion dollars of high interest debt. Some of the capital raised by the bond issue was used to buy the 50 percent of Industrial Finance Holdings that was owned by Scotia Bank. The reduction in interest costs was replaced by a foreign exchange risk. The bonds would only be repaid if the subsidiaries were profitable, which depended on the Jamaican economy and market conditions being favorable to the subsidiaries' operations.

But the Jamaican economy in 1996 was on the brink of disaster. Jamaica experienced the virtual collapse of its financial sector, a situation that had been, in retrospect, in train for the previous five years. Due to a number of factors, but largely the liberalization of the financial sector and the speculative behavior of weakly regulated financial institutions, the Jamaican crash echoed that of Mexico in 1994. In terms of percentage of GDP it was actually worse.

In July 1996, in an attempt to stem a run on Century National Bank, one of the first Jamaican-owned commercial banks, and to forestall a domino effect, the government took charge of its assets. This signaled the beginning of the largest financial sector crisis in Jamaica's history. To protect depositors, the government took control of the majority of Jamaica's financial institutions—banks, insurance companies and building societies. The eventual cost of the bailout was 40 percent of GDP, the largest bailout of a financial sector in the world, making Jamaica one of the three most indebted countries in the world. Among the outcomes were the closure of many businesses, the devaluation of the Jamaican dollar, and an economic recession that saw a 4 percent fall in output between 1995–1999.

This was the context in which Mechala had issued its fixed-rate bonds in US currency. By the end of 1998 it became clear that, with the subsidiaries not having performed as expected and not having generated sufficient revenue, Mechala would not be able to pay out the bondholders by the bonds' maturity date in 1999. Mayer Matalon was faced with the most excruciating dilemma of his life. His father had been forced to declare bankruptcy, something that Mayer and his brothers had considered such a stain on their family's name that Aaron and Mayer had, twenty years after their father's death, taken steps to pay off the debt and get the bankruptcy discharged. Mayer's lawyer and friend, Pat Rousseau, whom they commissioned to do this, said that in fifty-five years of practicing law in Jamaica this was the only time he had ever known of such an action.

The solution proposed for the Mechala bonds, a "scheme of arrangement"—a court-sanctioned compromise or agreement between a company in financial distress and its creditors—was too close to a declaration of bankruptcy for

Mayer. He agreed to it only after extensive discussion and a great deal of persuasion, and even then extremely reluctantly; the fact is that there was no other viable option. The scheme of arrangement provided for Mechala to repay the bondholders US$0.57 on the dollar with an additional two million US dollars as a consent payment.

To get to an agreement on this settlement was the last, the most arduous, and the most unpleasant negotiation of Mayer Matalon's life. Mayer, and his son Joe M., felt very strongly that no Jamaican creditor should suffer as a result of the restructuring and the failure of the bond issue. The only bondholders to be affected were sophisticated, institutional investors who had taken a calculated risk. This was as much a practical position as a sentimental one: if a significant proportion of local lenders, investors and creditors had lost out, it would have been difficult for Mayer, Joe and the rest of the family to continue to live in Jamaica.

The negotiations with the creditors' committee were long and drawn out. When it came to a point where it looked like a stalemate, the Matalons offered to appoint creditor representatives to the board as a majority. This offer was made with the caveat that they be allowed to undertake an orderly liquidation of the business rather than bring the axe down and fire sale the assets, and that local creditors not be affected. At that point, the creditors' committee realized that the fifty-seven cents offer was the best possible outcome.

They had to come up with US$57 million. A loan of US$20 million from Scotia Bank was made possible by Mayer's long and close relationship with the bank. Family members who held bonds were not paid. Mayer was the only shareholder among the siblings who had accumulated significant wealth independent of the family business, and was therefore able to put up the necessary equity as a loan, with a lien on their shares as security.

The failure of the Mechala initiative took a toll on Mayer, exacerbated by the ensuing fallout with his brothers and some of their children. Many of them blamed him bitterly for what had happened, splitting the family even further. Mayer, who had always worked in the family's interest, felt misunderstood and unappreciated. There was disagreement as to the direction ICD should take. Aaron, who had hitherto stood solidly beside Moses and Mayer, turned against Mayer. It transpired that Aaron considered he himself, not Mayer, was the brain behind ICD, and that Mayer was destroying what he had built. For his part, Mayer felt he had dedicated his entire life, and sacrificed his own personal ambitions, to the success of both the family and family business. He was chagrined that his efforts to support family members, whether by directly paying their living expenses, quietly bailing them out in times of need, investing in their ventures (often at a loss), and unscrupulously offering them stakes in his own investments, which he did all the work toward, were forgotten in the rush to judge him as greedy and selfish.

Figure 9.1. Mayer with his son Joe M., early 2000s
Photo courtesy of Joseph M. Matalon.

From 2000–2005, with Mayer's son Joe M. (fig. 9.1) now the majority shareholder, chairman and CEO of ICD, all of the manufacturing, trading and distribution subsidiaries were either liquidated or divested. The staff complement was restructured and significantly downsized, with most of the Matalon family members who had worked in ICD or WIHCON losing their jobs. ICD's main interests shifted to financial services and WIHCON had moved from large-scale, low-income housing scheme projects to smaller scale, upper-income developments. The WIHCON building system was no longer in use, and other developers filled the gap in the Jamaican housing market with similar low-cost building systems. Mayer was involved in all the decisions regarding the restructuring; when he wasn't in Jamaica he and Joe spoke every day on the phone.

Around this time, Sarita developed early-onset Alzheimer's and declined rapidly, to the point where she didn't recognize Mayer. Vernon, the baby brother to whom he had grown very close, and who had sided with Mayer in the family divide, died in 2006. In the face of these setbacks, Mayer and Sarita relocated to Panama, where they moved into an apartment two floors up from their daughter Rebeca. While Rebeca thought of herself as their caregiver, Mayer saw himself as caregiver to Sarita: "She looked after me all my life, now it's my turn to look after her."[1]

Life in Panama did not suit Mayer. He found its Jewish community—ostensibly his natural enclave given Sarita's and Rebeca's family ties—insular and closed. Despite its surface acceptance, perhaps he was reminded of the subtle and not-so-subtle exclusion that he and his brothers faced as young men, before they had "made it" and were acknowledged by the Jamaican Jewish elite. The only thing he liked about Panama, he often said, was the *guayaberas*, the elegant white linen shirts that he favored. He loved Jamaica and returned regularly, especially for BNS board meetings. In Panama his quality of life deteriorated further after a heart attack, which he survived only because he was already at the hospital being checked for chest pain.

For Mayer his final years were marked by a paradoxical mix of profound disappointments and pride in the comeback engineered by Joe M., with him in the wings. That ICD's renewal was led by his own son, who he had mentored through his formative years as a businessman, brought him tremendous gratification. But the split in the family brought about by Mechala's foundering troubled him deeply. He had not resolved his differences with Aaron by the time of Aaron's passing in 2009. By then, only he and Owen remained of the original sibling group; their relationship also remained unresolved.

For a man accustomed to positions of power, the waning of his influence and political access was a source of discontent. He was particularly disillusioned that despite his decades of advising prime ministers and ministers of finance, neither his warnings nor his recommendations were heeded. The failure of the Mechala initiative to do what it was intended to was in large part due to the crisis, so he felt its consequences directly. Beyond his personal family business interests, the damage to the Jamaican economy and national development was devastating. Years later, the same people who had not heeded his counsel acknowledged that, had Mayer Matalon been listened to, the fallout from the financial sector crisis and the massive damage that ensued could have been forestalled and contained. Had his advice been followed, his erstwhile critics agreed, it would have been his most significant contribution to public policy in his lifetime, surpassing even the NHT and the bauxite negotiations.

In 2010 Mayer and his children decided that he and Sarita should move back to Jamaica, the country he loved and the place he felt most at home. He resumed going to the office at Harbour Street, where a chair lift for the steep, winding staircase was installed for him, and where he kept busy. By this time, the seeds of resurgence that his son Joseph M., who was now the majority shareholder in ICD, had planted were starting to blossom. Mayer took no small amount of satisfaction in the fact that ICD, even if now no longer the family business that it had started as, nor the business that the Mechala initiative had intended, was in the process of being restored to profitability and growth, and was successfully moving into new and innovative businesses and sectors that crossed international borders and harnessed new technologies. ICD was being renewed into a global, twenty-first century entity in a way that few other Jamaican businesses had or have managed to accomplish. He was proud of Joe's own success in public service and growing influence in policy decision making, and delighted in advising him whenever asked. A year and a half later he died, peacefully, at his home on Long Lane.

NOTE

1. Interview with Matalon family member, April 29, 2017.

Chapter Ten

The World of Mayer Matalon

The Matalon name went from a "herring Jew" to being the by-word for wealth in Jamaica in one generation. From the 1950s to the 1990s "Matalon" was to Jamaica what "Rockefeller" was to the United States. Theirs was a corporation whose growth and reach have few rivals in Jamaican history, and many of their ventures changed the face of Jamaica, introducing low cost housing that made home ownership a reality for tens of thousands of Jamaicans, and literally creating parts of the island that today we take for granted: Portmore, Ocho Rios, Newport West. The Matalon story would be compelling in any context of a "rags to riches" tale of business success.

But the Matalons' influence went beyond business, as they were deeply involved in politics and government policy and action over many decades. Among the sibling group some of the brothers stood out for their prominent positions as heads of powerful public bodies and industry associations, and their high profile political involvement: Zackie was appointed to independent Jamaica's first senate, and was later custos of St. Thomas; Eli held an elected office and a cabinet position; Moses' engineering feats brought about critical infrastructure landmarks beyond Jamaica into the Eastern Caribbean; Aaron established the first professional training institution in the island. Michael Manley went so far as to say: "The Matalon family is undoubtedly one of the most remarkable families in *Caribbean history.*"[1]

Amidst this remarkable family of high achievers, Mayer was *primus inter pares*. Mayer's influence went the furthest, in business, and in government policy. His role in the family business was key to its remarkable growth and success; he had the deepest and most extensive political reach—advising and in some cases being a critical balancing force to every Jamaican prime minister from the 1950s to the 2000s, with only one exception, and introducing transformative ideas that the state successfully pursued; and his leadership of two of the most powerful multinational companies in Jamaica had profound impacts on Jamaica and its development.

The inevitable question is: How does one man go from sharing a pair of pants with his brother, to personally brokering the government's paybill on the Friday before Christmas? What were the personal qualities that led to political leaders wanting to hear what he thought, especially about economic and financial matters, and to large multinational corporations trusting him to carry their Jamaican business forward? And how did that combination of personality and influence manifest?

Mayer Matalon had many qualities which have already been enumerated within these pages: his wit, his gift for numbers, his ingenuity, his bawdy humor, his confidence, his integrity, and even his intransigence, are remembered and recounted with affection by almost everyone who crossed his path. One might say Mayer possessed extraordinary emotional intelligence—the capacity to be aware of, control, and express one's emotions appropriately, and to handle interpersonal relationships judiciously and empathetically. But there are other attributes which are not so obvious, which are key to understanding how Mayer came to play the crucial roles that were so transformative for Jamaica.

Key to virtually all of the exploits and achievements explored in this book, was Mayer's ability to invest in and leverage social capital. Social capital comprises resources, like influence, wealth, power and status, embedded in a social structure; these may be accessed, utilized, leveraged and expanded by an individual's investment in relationships with other individuals, within a social network. Successfully leveraging one's social capital not only increases one's own social capital, but also allows the individual to claim additional resources of information, influence, and the esteem of others.[2]

Mayer no doubt recognized and began to exploit this gift of understanding how social capital worked when he was a teenager, as a scholarship boy at Jamaica College. As a white-skinned student at Jamaica College, one of the most prestigious boys' schools in Jamaica, among the privileged white and light brown sons of the Jamaican business elite, Mayer would have absorbed their behavioral norms. At a time when education was restricted to the sons and daughters of the elite, the relationships and acquaintances he formed at Jamaica College situated him in the Jamaican upper class, his own family's circumstances notwithstanding. There, among boys far better off than himself, he would have recognized that there were other resources he could access, employ, leverage, and build on, resources innate to himself. His friendships at Jamaica College would have been the first arena in which he would have invested that social capital; these relationships would come to have significant implications for his social standing and access to power.

Mayer's acumen with numbers, and his charisma, were augmented by another valuable endowment, important in colonial Jamaica: whiteness. Being white in the mid-twentieth century in a colonial island nation such as Jamaica, where a majority black population was subservient to a white ruling elite, was a source of tremendous power. The social construct of race, class and privilege that evolves from such a social hierarchy, automatically grants power to any white-skinned or "near-white" person (someone of mixed race with fair skin and/or straight hair and/or phenotypically "white" facial features), once their behavior and manner of speaking (the correct accent and correct use of English) conform to the elite's norms and expectations. Entering the world of work in Jamaica as a young white man with the appropriate manners and commensurate accent, regardless of qualifications, he would have been guaranteed a job with an employer, who would undoubtedly then look for opportunities to advance him.

It is often assumed that Mayer being Jewish endowed him with some sort of automatic privilege, in the context of the Jamaican Jewish elite that held enormous political and economic power in the Jamaica that he was born into. But Mayer wasn't the right sort of Jamaican Jew, not at first. Up until he and his brothers began to reap some business success, he was an outsider, excluded from any natural advantage that might have been accorded him by the mere fact of being born to Jewish parents. In fact Mayer could be said to be an accidental member of the Jewish Jamaican elite, who at first snubbed him and his "hurry-come-up" brothers. Around the time the siblings came together and established Commodity Services Company in 1946, three of Mayer Matalon's seven brothers married daughters of establishment Jamaican Jewish families. These were love marriages, the first of which, Aaron to Marjorie DeMercado, was a minor scandal in Jewish Jamaican circles. It was unheard of for the son of a Syrian Jew and a "nobody Jew," who himself didn't complete high school, to marry the daughter of an established Jewish Jamaican family. The scandal, however, was short-lived; shortly afterwards, Zackie, the eldest Matalon son, met Evelyn Henriques, née Mordecai, daughter of another prominent, landed Jewish family, on a visit to St. Thomas with his brother and new sister-in-law. They married. By the time Moses married Barbara DeMercado, his sister-in-law Marjorie's sister, a few years later, it was not even remarkable.

Ironically, perhaps, his Jewishness did serve him well in later years, by which time he would undoubtedly have been in the elite, with making contacts with other elite Jews in the United States and the United Kingdom. But at the core Mayer was a Jamaican who rose, through upward social and economic mobility, to join the Jamaican socio-economic elite, and he happened to be a Jew, in a context where a powerful Jewish Jamaican elite was deeply entrenched. There was a point where his Jewishness was something of a social disadvantage in the Jamaica of the British colonial elites, but in the rapidly changing social context of newly independent Jamaica, this mattered less and less very quickly. This society in transition was where Mayer and his siblings seized the opportunities that made them wealthy and famous in Jamaica, and in which they made their indelible mark.

Mayer and his brothers also defied their Jewishness, as it was typically manifested in colonial and post-colonial Jamaica, with their political ideas and affiliations. They would have been the only Jewish-Jamaican support for the People's National Party in the 1940s and 1950s—at a time when Norman Manley had declared the PNP a socialist party, and stated that "all the means of production should in one form or the other come to be publicly owned and controlled,"[3] as well as the only significant support from a prominent business family. This was not because they were iconoclastic, but because they were not born into the Jewish-Jamaican wealthy class and thus had no land or interests to defend.

These political connections, established from the late 1940s through Mayer's older brothers' friendships and relationships with the upper echelons of the PNP, were critical elements of the family's prominence and business success. Norman Manley, Florizel Glasspole, David Coore, and Eric Bell, stalwarts of the PNP in the 1940s and 1950s, were among Eli, Moses and Aaron's close associates. They paved the way for Mayer to establish his own ties in the party, ties which became entrenched in the ensuing decades, with Mayer's influence at an apex in both of Michael Manley's administrations.

The deep ties to and embeddedness in the uppermost echelons of the PNP did not necessarily equal access or favors that no one else was privy to. What it did was allow for a deep understanding and familiarity with government policies, which, together with the Matalons' entrepreneurial instincts, and particularly with Mayer's skill in seeing the financial angle in just about any situation, meant that the Matalons were able to hone in on opportunities, and pursue endeavours, that would not have been obvious to many others. Their ability to network with government officials at all levels crossed party lines, and though they were expressly PNP, JLP leaders and governments did not shut them out or allow any obstacles to their businesses' continued growth and expansion.

The Matalons' interwovenness with the PNP's decision-making cadre had far more profound implications than simply giving the Matalons an edge in their business dealings. As the only significant capitalist voice in the PNP's early days, their influence is quite likely what led Norman Manley to follow a more moderate capitalistic path, with an economic policy that was mostly focused on import substitution industrialization, than his stated intention to completely change "the basic organisation of the social and economic conditions," so as to render Jamaica a place "in which all opportunities will be equal and open to all persons; such a state of affairs cannot exist under a society organised on capitalist lines."[4]

Mayer and his brothers, however, were not only capitalists, they were nationalists. Mayer would, in the 1970s, quite literally, walk the talk of a Jamaican who was truly dedicated to his country, when he chose to stay while everyone around him was leaving the island. The Matalons believed that Jamaica was ripe with opportunity for business, but they understood that business had a social responsibility to ensure that wealth was shared, at the same time as they recognized, supported, and promoted the imperative for the state to take deliberate action to reduce poverty and increase economic and social opportunities for the majority poor Jamaicans.

For half a century, the Matalon name was perhaps more widely known, and more often identified with wealth and power, than any other in Jamaica. Into the 2020s, Jamaicans born after the Matalons' heyday, who probably couldn't identify who they were or anything they did, still associate the name with affluence, perhaps because the name has been kept alive in the popular culture in this vein. In 2019 the name remains a strong enough brand that a con man in New York City was able to swindle people out of hundreds of thousands of dollars by claiming that he was a Matalon.[5]

The name took such a hold because the Matalons captured the imagination of the Jamaican public. From early in their foray into business, the Matalon brothers were portrayed in the media, and considered by many, their peers included, as having "the golden touch." Some of their ventures were ambitious and original. The wide scope of their business activities meant that over four decades they employed tens of thousands of Jamaicans. Their housing ventures, particularly in the construction of homes for lower and middle income Jamaicans, gave their name a familiarity far beyond that of any other businessperson in Jamaica. How Mayer secured the mortgage financing for their first housing projects was itself groundbreaking, and brought him wide and admiring acclaim. In the effort to restructure the business, their last major initiative, the idea of attempting an initial public offering on the international capital markets was a first for any Jamaican company. Their subsequent success with a bond issue on the international markets was also a first.

Starting from nothing, the Matalon brothers' entrepreneurial instinct led the family business to rapid growth and expansion, and for some three decades, profits to catapult the family, all eleven of them, to the upper middle class. They identified gaps in the market and entered market segments early, they pursued business ventures that no one else had thought to explore, and accessed capital from previously untapped sources. Much of this success was due to Mayer's proficiency with numbers, his negotiating skills, and his persistence in pursuing outsized ambitions; but he was buttressed by his siblings and their own unique strengths.

For thirty years, their businesses grew along with the Jamaican economy. Their distribution enterprise and their manufacturing businesses were in protected sectors, enjoying little competition in a sheltered market. The really pathbreaking large-scale projects in housing and dredging were massive undertakings, in terms of physical scope, magnitude of financing, and logistics of planning and implementation. These projects were ambitious and far-reaching, and largely unfeasible for the less endowed and less connected due to their scope, the capital needed to see them off the ground and through to completion, and the involvement of the state at many steps along the way, with regard to land acquisition, permits and approvals, and the like.

The 1970s was a critical juncture for the business. During their fourth decade in business, changes in the external environment destabilized the foundation of what was by then a conglomerate, and threatened its success. The 1970s was a punishing decade for most Jamaican businesses. The economy contracted, GDP fell, direct investment diminished, public spending increased, the debt burden multiplied, and many managers and skilled workers left the island. Inflammatory anti-business rhetoric was rife in the political discourse.

At the same time, the family dynamic was in flux. If we consider Joseph who arrived in Jamaica in 1910 as the first generation of Matalons, the third generation would be the offspring of Mayer, Aaron, and Moses and their siblings. These third-generation Matalon children were now of age to work in the business, and some of them joined ICD, or one of its subsidiaries. Some had studied disciplines in college that were suited to specific aspects of the business, while positions were found for others regardless of their training or qualifications.

The political, social and economic instability pushed many of the Matalon siblings and their families to leave Jamaica. Mayer did not want to leave, and resented those who did. There was no longer a full complement of siblings managing day-to-day, and those overseas relied on the business to continue supporting them; a large proportion of the dwindling profits went towards that, rather than being reinvested in the businesses. The business grew weaker and simultaneously the fractures in the family surfaced, deepened, and widened.

Little of this was apparent outside of the family. The Matalons presented themselves at the outset as a family unit, working in harmony. They were a picture-perfect group, each with his or her expert niche: one good at numbers, one a marketing expert, one an engineer, one a good manager, and so on.

Each complemented the other as they harnessed their strengths and differences towards a common goal: an uncommon combination of a commitment to business success and to national development. Many family businesses portray themselves like this—that fate gave them the perfect combination of siblings to be a united force. While not always completely untrue, it is more often an aspirational ideal. They persisted with this story, through the difficult decades of the 1980s and 1990s.

Family stories are seldom simple, even less so with families that are in business together. The family business where everyone gets along harmoniously all the time is rare. More commonly, childhood slights become adult grievances, and sibling and cousin rivalries become divisive jealousy. Who is being paid how much and on what basis looms large and destructive in the psyche of those who feel they ought to be paid more. The question of who got more hugs from mum, or whose birthday party had more balloons, turns into whose house is bigger than whose, or who is driving a newer, bigger car; they become matters of insidious envy, often pushed under the carpet to fester. The larger the family, the more prospect there is for discord. The details will vary from one business family to another, but this is a universal narrative, not unique to the Matalons, not unique to any one family in any one place.

As the Jamaican political and economic climate stabilized and evolved in the 1980s and into the 1990s, the business continued to struggle. Changing import policies made the traditional manufacturing sector less viable. Domestic markets changed in size, preferences, and purchasing power. The external economy shrank and stagnated. Global trade agreements changed the terms of trade. All of these led to a decline in revenues, and a heavy debt burden. Onerous and rising domestic interest rates kept the businesses from being able to reinvest, adapt to the new market conditions, innovate, or become more competitive.

The instability in the family remained. The Matalons' abundance of heirs, the third generation, counted among them some talented leaders. But, combined with a patriarchal line of succession in which the few women who worked in the business did not take prominent leadership roles, they were not enough to continue the business as a broadly held family concern, not in the context of the dispersal of the family outside of Jamaica, and the rifts that had deepened as the business's foundation weakened. Non-family high-level talent was not brought in early.

Within the third generation, particularly those in the business, conflicts developed between cousins over perceived favoritism and slights, nurturing resentments that filtered up to their parents, and exacerbated the extant tensions. It is extremely difficult for family businesses to avoid this kind of conflict. The same differences that promote synergies in their joint efforts as they build the business can turn into bitter disputes when those differences, for whatever reason, no longer yield positive results. Even if the original sibling group is able to manage its own interpersonal relationships successfully, once spouses and then children join the family, and especially if they join the business, fights are inevitable, and unless anticipated and handled with extreme care and sensitivity, can be destructive. An individual family member, if so motivated, can wreak havoc with whisper campaigns and the like, exacerbating the innate fault lines of any family.

A second critical juncture occurred in the mid-1990s, with the restructuring attempt. That effort was not, despite surface appearances, in line with a typical family business trajectory, where seventy percent of family-owned businesses fail before the next generation can take over.[6] Those who bought into the neat story line that the creation of Mechala in 1996 represented a handing of the baton to the next generation, and the convenient suggestion that Mayer's position as chairman of Mechala was a type of emeritus or honorary position, were oblivious to the absence of a clear delineation between the generations, and also to the fact that Mayer and his brothers were still involved at various levels of decision making. They might interpret the fact that the Matalon business empire began its demise after Mayer's son, Joseph M., and Aaron's son, Joseph A., ostensibly took over the helm, as proof that this amounted to an unsuccessful intergenerational transfer.

Business is seldom so straightforward and family businesses even less so. The overriding fact is that the business was in trouble, and the external environment had immutably transformed, far apart from any consideration of intergenerational transfer. The role of Mayer's and Aaron's sons as principals in the restructuring attempt was not the cause of its failure, nor did the demise have much to do with their generation. By the time the family took measures to save the business the problems ran very deep. The timing was terrible, coinciding with a virtual meltdown of the Jamaican economy, which experienced one of the most severe banking and financial crises in the world. The risky, Herculean effort at rescue couldn't and didn't save it—at least not as it was intended. The family was similarly fated. The original entity persisted after it was dramatically restructured, but was it was no longer a broadly held family business, and the Matalon family was no longer the overarching business power that it once had been.

One hundred and ten years after Joseph Matalon made his way from Mexico to Kingston, his descendants are mostly in North America, some in South America and Europe. Few of the third generation live in Jamaica, and some have no contact with the island or their remaining family on it. ICD is almost entirely in the hands of Mayer's son, Joe M., who, by all appearances, has successfully reinvented the conglomerate into a 21st century business. The

Matalon name is still culturally powerful, even though it's quite possible that anyone born since 2000 doesn't know where it originated; and the twenty-one families idea still holds currency and is kept alive with uncritical references in books, and bandied about in university lecture rooms.

But Mayer's story was not only the story of his family, and the family business was not Mayer's only business, neither literally nor figuratively. Apart from ICD, WIHCON, and the subsidiaries, Mayer maintained deep involvement with other businesses that he chaired, and led to great successes, namely the Bank of Nova Scotia where he was *de facto* chairman, and later Telecommunications of Jamaica/Cable and Wireless, as well as pursued his own business ventures, many of which were fruitful.

His role as a political insider, especially as Michael Manley's close confidante, is also significant. Behind the scenes he acted as a counter balance to Manley and Jamaica being tugged leftwards. When there was a break between them, he waited on the sidelines. During the 1980s Mayer was Manley's chief sounding board, and he personally supported Manley and the PNP through those difficult years, after which Manley, rehabilitated, returned to power.

Through his seminal role in the family's businesses, as chairman of other significant Jamaican entities, his relationships with Jamaica's most powerful politicians and leaders, his role as advisor on economic and financial policy, and his positions in some of the most critical negotiations between the Jamaican government and multinational corporations over some fifty years, Mayer Matalon has earned a place in the pantheon of Jamaican business titans.

There will never be another Mayer Matalon in Jamaica—someone whose influence spans so many sectors, and over such a long period of time—because Jamaica and the world have changed, and modern norms of governance and of propriety no longer accommodate the discretionary power of a single person in that way. Mention Mayer Matalon's name to any Jamaican familiar with business or politics and born before 1962, and even to some born later, and their face softens and their eyes shine. Everyone has a story to tell about Mayer. The fondness and awe with which he is remembered is a tribute to the unique, exceptional person that he was.

NOTES

1. Ferguson, "The Matalons," 23. Italics are my emphasis.
2. Nan Lin, "Building a Network Theory of Social Capital," *Connections* 22, no.1 (1999): 28–51, www.insna.org/PDF/Connections/v22/1999_I-1-4.pdf.
3. Paul Burke, "Norman Manley's concept of socialism," *Observer*, July 16, 2016, www.jamaicaobserver.com/columns/Norman-Manley-s-concept-of-socialism_66842.

4. Burke, ibid.

5. Rebecca Rosenberg and Sarah Trefethen, "Con man scammed investors over $100K at swanky Manhattan parties," *New York Post*, January 6, 2019, https://nypost.com/2019/01/06/con-man-scammed-investors-over-100k-at-swanky-manhattan-parties/.

6. Scott James, "Losing a Fortune Often Comes Down to One Thing: Family," *New York Times*, February 19, 2017, www.nytimes.com/2017/02/19/your-money/losing-a-fortune-often-comes-down-to-one-thing-family.html?mcubz=3.

Postscript

The legend of Jamaica's "twenty-one families" comes to my mind often, not because of who was on this list of the supposed most powerful people in Jamaica in the mid-1970s, but because it is a vivid example of how an idea can so take hold that, regardless of whether or not it is factual, it becomes a truth unto itself. In the case of the "twenty-one families" list, it has become a critical data point for a racialized and politicized belief system that has dominated the Jamaican intellectual discourse with regard to the country's development, a discourse that is constantly revealed as inconsistent, partisan, and even hypocritical by those willing to challenge the received orthodoxy. These shibboleths forestall us coming to terms with the reality of our complex, sometimes uncomfortable history, and so preclude feasible, grounded solutions.

Emblematic of this dichotomy is the place of the Matalon family on that list. Of the "twenty-one families," seven were Jewish, and four of those were particularly powerful given the number of directorships they occupied, according to the essay's metric. The Matalons were one of that four. But having been lumped into that group with the Henriques, the Ashenheims, and the deCordovas—storied Jewish families who had been in Jamaica for generations—the Matalons' very different origins became obscured, and thenceforth, with the exception of the few who scratched beneath the surface, were subsumed into the story of the Jamaican Jewish gentry, and the true story was lost. But those origins are intriguing, and different; they provide a unique and exotic twist to the typical Jamaican rags to riches story.

As a newspaper-reading child growing up in Jamaica I was aware of the Matalon name and legacy—a large, successful, influential Jewish Jamaican family, in the tradition of the Jamaican Jews of lore; I never thought to question the conventional wisdom. But after I married into a large business family, which was an entirely new world for me having come from a family of professionals, I grew curious about the stories of family businesses, and about the truth behind the stereotypes.

My husband, Wayne Chen, encouraged me to explore that curiousity in the context of my ongoing unsettledness with the status quo that accepts and reifies facile untruths, and from that starting point this book was conceptualized. We identified Mayer Matalon as the ideal subject, given his outsize persona, his extraordinary political influence, and his fascinating but little-known origin story. His story crossed so many different dimensions of Jamaican life—business, politics, our ethnographic history—that it was in many ways a lens through which one could look at the Jamaican story itself.

We often lament in Jamaica that we don't tell our own stories enough. The accounts of our people and our history are dominated by academics with ideological perspectives and language that don't necessarily tell the stories that Jamaicans long for, or that aren't accessible, and so the stories get lost along the way. My goal with this book is to contribute to the growing body of memoirs and biographies about important and interesting Jamaicans, and to provide an alternative view to the dominant single story, with a view to bringing us all to a better understanding of our country and ourselves.

Sources

Mayer Matalon left no personal papers of any sort. With the exception of some aspects of chapter two, this book is comprised entirely of information gathered from interviews, from newspaper and news magazine articles, books, and academic articles, most of which are included in the bibliography.

I read widely to broaden and deepen my understanding of the economic, political and historical context of Mayer Matalon's life; the appendix "Further Reading" contains a complete list of published materials that were not cited but which provided me with information that helped me to better understand and frame the information I gathered from my research.

For much of the unreferenced information I relied heavily on Ainsley Henriques and his mother, Evelyn Matalon. Ainsley Henriques is a Jewish Jamaican geneaologist; he became (Mayer's brother) Isaac "Zackie" Matalon's stepson when his mother, Evelyn, married Zackie in 1946. Mayer lived with Evelyn and Zackie for a couple of years, and they were close to Mayer and his wife Sarita throughout their lives. They provided me with information about Mayer as a young man, and details about the Jewish community in Jamaica in the early to mid-twentieth century that I could not have found elsewhere. Joseph M. Matalon, Mayer's son, Patrick Rousseau, Mayer's attorney and friend for many decades, and O. K. Melhado, Mayer's long-standing friend and later in-law, shared with me most of the other information in the book that is not cited. They also provided extensive feedback on various drafts of the manuscript, including providing details that were then incorporated into subsequent drafts.

Among the many gracious and helpful people who agreed to be interviewed were three of Mayer Matalon's daughters, the three people whom many of his family members described as his true friends, three former prime ministers, a former minister of finance, a former financial secretary, people who were close to both Michael Manley throughout the 1970s and who were also close associates of Mayer Matalon, and a number of people who had worked or otherwise interacted with Mayer Matalon at some period during his life. They all shared first-hand information on Mayer Matalon, some of which has been included in the book, some that provided me with contextual information, and some that deepened my understanding of circumstances that are relayed in the book. My sense from the interviews was that people would speak more freely if they were not directly quoted or if information was not directly attributed to them, hence there are only a few instances where interviewees are named.

I also benefitted from many informal conversations I had over a three-year period with various people who worked with or knew Mayer Matalon, or who were otherwise in his orbit, and who shared anecdotes or tidbits of information or insight that informed my understanding of events.

Appendix: Further Reading

Atkins, Fiona. "Financial Crises and Money Demand in Jamaica." Birkbeck Working Papers in Economics and Finance BWPEF 0512, 2005. www.bbk.ac.uk/ems/research/wp/PDF/BWPEF0512.pdf.

Caribbean Policy Research Institute. "An Assessment of the NHT." Kingston: CaPRI, 2016. www.capricaribbean.org/documents/assessment-nht-revised-july-2016.

Cassidy, Frederic G. and Robert Le Page. *Dictionary of Jamaican English.* Kingston: University of the West Indies Press, 2002.

Collister, Keith. "A Man of His Word: Mayer Matalon, 1922–2012." *Observer*, February 8, 2012. www.jamaicaobserver.com/business/A-man-of-his-word--Mayer-Matalon--1922---2012_10729918.

Cooper, Dereck W. "Migration from Jamaica in the 1970s: Political Protest or Economic Pull?" *The International Migration Review* 19, no. 4 (Winter 1985): 728–45.

Davis, Carlton E. "60 Years Of Bauxite Mining In Jamaica—Part I." *Gleaner*, June 5, 2012. www.jamaica-gleaner.com/gleaner/20120605/news/news1.html.

———. "60 Years of Bauxite Mining in Jamaica—Part II." *Gleaner*, June 6, 2012. www.jamaica-gleaner.com/gleaner/20120606/news/news1.html.

D'Costa, David. "A Talk with Aaron Matalon, Part 2." *Sunday Gleaner*, March 7, 1976.

Gleaner. "At Morant Bay. An Interesting Case Tried in the Resident Magistrate's Court. An Alien Enemy." December 23, 1914.

———. "Attention Shopkeepers" (advertisement). September 28, 1940.

———. "Before Court. Civil and Criminal Cases Heard Recently at Chapelton. The Position of Aliens." December 18, 1914.

———. "I.C.D.—It's a Long Road." July 27, 1975.

———. "ICD, BNS Form Joint Holding Company." November 24, 1988.

———. "Manufacturers Consider Boosting Exports to Sister Colonies." September 28, 1949.

———. "Midnight Attack on Matalons." June 8, 1975.

———. "Protest Resolution against Dr. Peat's Post Withdrawn." December 21, 1948.

———. "Turnbull Farm an Ideal Location for Thoroughbred Breeding." May 3, 1970.

Gordon, Peter-John. "The Jamaican Economy: Recent Developments and Prospects." *Souls* 3, no. 4 (Fall 2001): 22–31.

Hall, Douglas. *A Man Divided: M.G. Smith, Jamaican Poet and Anthropologist.* Kingston: University of the West Indies Press, 1997.

Jackson, Moses. "Business Leader Nominee #1—WIHCON." *Observer*, November 6, 2012. www.jamaicaobserver.com/business/Why-WIHCON-_12929890.

Klich, Ignacio. "Arab-Jewish Coexistence in the First Half of 1900s Argentina: Overcoming Self-Imposed Amnesia." In *Arabs and Jewish Immigrants in Latin America: Images and Realities*, edited by Ignacio Klich and Jeffrey Lesser, 1–37. London: Frank Cass, 1998.

Klich, Ignacio and Jeffrey Lesser. "Introduction: Images and Realities of Arab and Jewish Immigrants in Latin America." In *Arabs and Jewish Immigrants in Latin America: Images and Realities*, edited by Ignacio Klich and Jeffrey Lesser, vii–xiv. London: Frank Cass, 1998.

Lewis, Gordon K. *Growth of the Modern West Indies*. New York: Monthly Review Press, 1968.

Mandle, Jay. *Persistent Underdevelopment: Change and Economic Modernization in the West Indies*. New York: Routledge, 1996.

Moore, Brian L., and Michele A. Johnson. *"They do as they please": The Jamaican Struggle for Cultural Freedom after Morant Bay*. Kingston: University of the West Indies Press, 2011.

Moss-Solomon, James. "Jamaica and GraceKennedy: Dreams Converging, Roads Diverging." Kingston: GraceKennedy Foundation Annual Public Lecture, 2012.

Observer. "Why the NHT. Business Leader (Friends of the Private Sector) Award Nominee # 7." November 14, 2013. www.jamaicaobserver.com/business/Why-the-NHT_15432519.

Payne, Anthony. *Politics in Jamaica* (revised edition). Kingston: Ian Randle Publishers, 1994.

Persaude, Wilberne. *Jamaica Meltdown: Indigenous Financial Sector Crash*. Self-published: 1996.

Pryce, Everton. "The grip of corporate power." *Observer*, March 24, 2013. www.jamaicaobserver.com/columns/The-grip-of-corporate power_13918656?profile=&template=PrinterVersion.

Spike, Neville. "The Oligarchy and Privatization." *Gleaner*, February 2, 1992.

Stirton, Lindsay and Martin Lodge. *Embedding Regulatory Autonomy: The Reform of Jamaican Telecommunications Regulation, 1988–2001*. London: London School of Economics and Political Science Centre for the Analysis of Risk and Regulation, 2002. www.eprints.lse.ac.uk/35986/1/Disspaper5.pdf.

Stone, Carl. *Democracy and Clientelism in Jamaica*. Piscataway, NJ: Transaction Books, 1980.

Supreme Court of Jamaica. Judgment of Justice Sykes in Claim No. 2009 HCV 00070 between Joseph M. Matalon and Honourable Mayer Matalon O.J. v Jamaica Observer Limited. 2014.

———. Judgment of Justice Wolfe in Suit No. E469 of 1999 in the Matter of Section 192 of the Companies Act and in the Matter of Mechala Group Jamaica Limited. 2000.

Bibliography

Aldridge, Carl. "Non-Public Companies in the Matalon Group." *Money Index* 325, June 23, 1992.

August, Thomas G. "An Historical Profile of the Jewish Community of Jamaica." *Jewish Social Studies* 49, nos. 3/4 (Summer–Autumn 1987): 303–16.

Baugh, Edward. *Chancellor, I Present: A Collection of Convocation Citations Given at the University of the West Indies, Mona 1985–1998.* Kingston: University of the West Indies Press, 2000.

Blair, Colin. "What's to Become of Forum Hotel?" *Gleaner*, September 8, 1990.

Brown, Ingrid. "Mayor Says Close to 300,000 Living in Portmore, Not 182,000." *Observer*, June 18, 2013. www.jamaicaobserver.com/news/Census-wrong_14519318.

Bryan, Patrick. *Edward Seaga and the Challenges of Modern Jamaica*. Kingston: University of the West Indies Press, 2009.

Burke, Paul. "Norman Manley's concept of socialism." *Observer*, July 16, 2016. www.jamaicaobserver.com/columns/Norman-Manley-s-concept-of-socialism.

Daily Telegraph (UK). "How a Globe-Girdling Enterprise Snapped." February 1, 2006. www.telegraph.co.uk/finance/2931252/How-a-globe-girdling-enterprise-snapped.html.

Davies, Omar. Eulogy for Mayer Matalon, Shaare Shalom Synagogue, Kingston, Jamaica. February 7, 2012.

Davis, Carlton E. *Jamaica in the World Aluminium Industry Volume II—Bauxite Levy Negotiations, 1974–1988.* Kingston: Jamaica Bauxite Institute, 1989.

Delevante, Marilyn and Anthony Alberga. *The Island of One People. An Account of the History of the Jews of Jamaica.* Kingston: Ian Randle Publishers, 2006.

Dunn, Hopeton and Winston Gooden. "Telecommunications Policy Making in Jamaica: From State Monopoly to Private Monopoly." In *Telecommunications in Latin America*, edited by Eli Noam, 73–81. Oxford: Oxford University Press, 1997.

Ellington, Barbara. "William 'Bill' Clarke: 40 Years at the Number One Bank." *Gleaner*, May 18, 2008.

Fawcett, Louise and Eduardo Posada-Carbo. "Arabs and Jews in the Development of the Colombian Caribbean, 1850–1950." In *Arabs and Jewish Immigrants in Latin America: Images and Realities*, edited by Ignacio Klich and Jeffrey Lesser, 57–79. London: Frank Cass, 1994.

Ferguson, Elaine. "The Growth of an Empire—The Matalon Story." *Money Index* 323, no. 9 (June 1992): 21–50.

———. "The ICD Group—A Corporate Giant." *Money Index* 325, no. 23 (June 1992): 19–52.

———. "The Matalons." *Money Index* 324, no. 16 (June 1992): 19–48.

Gafar, John. "An Analysis of Import Substitution in a Developing Economy: The Case of Jamaica." *Caribbean Studies* 18, nos. 3–4 (Oct. 1978–Jan. 1979): 139–56.

Gleaner. "Govt. Buys Forum for Price Above Evaluators' Recommendation." October 30, 1982.

———. "Hosiery Co. Closing Down." September 30, 1988.

———. "House Approves Hughenden Housing Scheme." August 18, 1967.

———. "Miami-Kingston Air Race Suggested for Advertising Island." March 4, 1946.

———. "Service of Reconsecration at the Jewish Home." March 18, 1946.

———. "Seventh All-Island Dog Show Comes Off Successfully." July 8, 1949.

———. "There Are No Rights without Corresponding Responsibilities, Sir Neville tells JC boys." August 8, 1967.

———. "TOJ Buys Land from ICD Group." November 26, 1988.

———. "A Very Expensive Low-Cost Housing Scheme." January 21, 1989.

———. "Vivian Matalon to Head Theatre School." March 8, 1970.

Gray, Obika. *Radicalism and Social Change in Jamaica, 1960–1972*. Knoxville: University of Tennessee Press, 1991.

Hamilton, Howard. "Petroleum Industry in Chaos." *Gleaner*, November 27, 2016. www.jamaica-gleaner.com/article/focus/20161127/howard-hamilton-petroleum-industry-chaos.

Hamui-Halabe, Liz. "Re-creating Community: Christians from Lebanon and Jews from Syria in Mexico, 1900–1938." In *Arabs and Jewish Immigrants in Latin America: Images and Realities*, edited by Ignacio Klich and Jeffrey Lesser, 124–45. London: Frank Cass, 1994.

Henriques, Ainsley. "Mayer Michael Matalon: A Reflection and a Tribute." ICD Group website, 2012. www.icdgroup.net.

Holzberg, Carol S. *Minorities and Power in a Black Society: The Jewish Community of Jamaica*. Lanham, MD: The North-South Publishing Company, 1987.

Jamaica Chamber of Commerce. "The Matalon Family Success Story: A Living Example to all Jamaicans." *Jamaica Chamber of Commerce Journal* 33, no. 3 (September 1977): 11–13.

James, Scott. "Losing a Fortune Often Comes Down to One Thing: Family." *New York Times*, February 19, 2017. www.nytimes.com/2017/02/19/your-money/losing-a-fortune-often-comes-down-to-one-thing-family.html?mcubz=3.

King, Damien. "On the Origins of the Political Economy of Underdevelopment in Jamaica." Unpublished manuscript, 2013.

Knight, Franklin W. "The Crisis in the Contemporary Caribbean." *Contributions in Black Studies* 6, no. 2 (2008). https://scholarworks.umass.edu/cibs/vol6/iss1/2.

Laikin Elkin, Judith. *The Jews of Latin America.* New York: Holmes & Meier, 1998.

Levi, Darrell E. *Michael Manley: The Making of a Leader.* Kingston: Heinemann Caribbean, 1989.

Levy, Charles. *Hash and Roast Beef: A Memoir of Life as a Schoolboy at Jamaica College 1943–1949.* Spokane, WA: Griffin Publishers, 1995.

Lin, Nan. "Building a Network Theory of Social Capital." *Connections* 22, no.1 (1999): 28–51. www.insna.org/PDF/Connections/v22/1999_I-1-4.pdf.

Manley, Rachel. *In My Father's Shade: A Daughter's Insight into the Man Behind the Prime Minister's Mask.* Toronto: Alfred A. Knopf, 2000.

Mann, Fred. *A Drastic Turn of Destiny.* Toronto: Second Story Press, 2009.

Matalon, Aaron. "Growing up in Kingston." Twelfth Annual Bustamante Lecture, Kingston, Jamaica, February 26, 1998.

Matalon, Joseph M. "Remembrances of Dad." Eulogy for Mayer Matalon, Shaare Shalom Synagogue, Kingston, Jamaica, February 7, 2012.

Matalon, Mayer M. "The Management of Change." Speech delivered at luncheon of the Jamaican-American Chamber of Commerce, May 18, 1976. Kingston: Agency for Public Information, 1976.

Moore, Brian L., and Michele A. Johnson. *Neither Led nor Driven: Contesting British Cultural Imperialism in Jamaica, 1865–1920.* Kingston: University of the West Indies Press, 2004.

Mordecai, Martin. "Aaron Matalon (interview)." *Jamaica Journal* 19, no. 4 (1986): 11–18.

Morgan, Henley. "Dr Davies' Mea Culpa." *Observer*, October 25, 2002.

National Library of Jamaica. "History of Portmore." National Library of Jamaica website, 2015. www.nlj.gov.jm/history-notes/History%20of%20Portmore%20Final.pdf.

New York Times. "Jamaican Leader Seeking Minimum Price for Bauxite." June 4, 1975. www.nytimes.com/1975/06/04/archives/jamaican-leader-seeking-minimum-price-for-bauxite.html.

Newday. "Business: Another Matalon Milestone." Vol 7, no. 3 (March 1963).

———. "Jamaica." Vol. 1, no. 2 (September 1957).

Newman, Joanna. "Refugees from Nazism in the British Caribbean." In *The Jews in the Caribbean*, edited by Jane S. Gerber, 343–59. Portland, OR: The Littman Library of Jewish Civilization, 2014.

Nicholls, David. "No Hawkers and Pedlars: Arabs of the Antilles." In *Haiti in Caribbean Context: Ethnicity, Economy, and Revolt*, edited by David Nicholls, 135–64. Oxford: Oxford, 1985.

Observer. "Business Process Outsourcing Carrying the Swing: Let's Go for It!" January 12, 2016. www.jamaicaobserver.com/editorial/Business-Process-Outsourcing-carrying-the-swing--Let-s-go-for-it-_48498.

———. "St. Lucia Names Causeway in Honour of Moses Matalon," August 17, 2015. www.jamaicaobserver.com/news/St-Lucia-names-causeway-in-honour-of-Moses-Matalon_19224144.

Orme, William A. "Israel Seen as a Paradise for Money Laundering." *New York Times*, February 21, 2000. www.nytimes.com/2000/02/21/world/israel-seen-as-paradise-for-money-laundering.html.

Palmer, Colin A. *Freedom's Children: The 1938 Labour Rebellion and the Birth of Modern Jamaica*. Kingston: Ian Randle Publishers, 2014.

Patterson, P. J. *My Political Journey: Jamaica's Sixth Prime Minister*. Kingston: University of the West Indies Press, 2018.

Private Sector Organization of Jamaica, Citation to Mayer Matalon on his Admission to the PSOJ Hall of Fame, 1994.

Reid, Stanley. "An Introductory Approach to the Concentration of Power in the Jamaican Corporate Economy and Notes on Its Origin." In *Essays on Power and Change in Jamaica*, edited by Carl Stone and Aggrey Brown, 15–44. Kingston: Jamaica Publishing House, 1977.

Robinson, Gordon. "Mayer Matalon—Jamaica's 'Chairman of the Board.'" *Gleaner*, July 22, 2012. www.new.jamaica-gleaner.com/gleaner/20120722/focus/focus6.html.

Rousseau, Patrick. "Tribute." Eulogy for Mayer Matalon, Shaare Shalom Synagogue, Kingston, Jamaica, February 7, 2012.

Seaga, Edward. *My Life and Leadership Volume II: Hard Road to Travel 1980–2008*. Oxford: Macmillan, 2010.

Shearer, Hugh Lawson. "New Year's Message." January 1, 1970. www.rjrnewsonline.com/archive/new-years-message-1970-prime-minister-hugh-lawson-shearer.

Smith, Godfrey. *Michael Manley: The Biography*. Kingston: Ian Randle Publishers, 2016.

Thorburn, Diana. "Nationalism, Identity and the Banking Sector: The English-speaking Caribbean in the Era of Financial Globalization." In *Ethnicity, Race and Nationalism in the Caribbean*, edited by Anton Allahar, 57–84. New York: Lexington Press, 2005.

Treaster, Joseph B. "Jamaica, Close U.S. Ally, Does Little to Halt Drugs." *New York Times*, September 10, 1984. www.nytimes.com/1984/09/10/world/jamaica-close-us-ally-does-little-to-halt-drugs.html?pagewanted=all.

Tortello, Rebecca. *Pieces of the Past: A Stroll Down Jamaica's Memory Lane*. Kingston: Ian Randle Publishers, 2007.

US Embassy, Kingston. Telegram 253 to the Department of State, Washington DC, January 19, 1976. www.history.state.gov/historicaldocuments/frus1969-76ve11p1/d459.

Varon, Benno Weiser. *Professions of a Lucky Jew*. New York: Cornwall Books, 1992.

WIHCON. "History." WIHCON website, 2017. www.wihcon.com/history.

Wint, Alvin G. "Has the Obsolescing Bargain Obsolesced? Negotiating with Foreign Investors." In *International Business and Government Relations in the 21st Century*, edited by Robert Grosse, 315–38. Cambridge: Cambridge University Press, 2011.

Wray, Richard. 2010. "Ten Years after the Crash, the Dotcom Boom can Finally Come of Age." *Guardian* (UK), March 14, 2010. www.theguardian.com/business/2010/mar/14/technology-dotcom-crash-2000.

Wray, Richard and Jill Treanor. "High Price of C&W Salvation." *Guardian* (UK), January 11, 2003. www.theguardian.com/business/2003/jan/11/4.
Younkin, Peter. "An American Oligopoly: How the American Pharmaceutical Industry Transformed Itself during the 1940s." Paper presented at the annual meeting of the American Sociological Association, New York, August 11, 2007. www.citation.allacademic.com/meta/p_mla_apa_research_citation/1/8/4/4/1/pages184412/p184412-1.php.

Index

accusations, 56
advice, 4; experience and, 28; foresight and, 96; politics and, 86
advocacy, 91
airplanes, 32
Allen, Edwin, 28; rebuttal to, 32
aluminum, 75
Alzheimer's disease, 104
ambitions, 31; sacrifice for, 102
Amin, Idi, 80
ANSA Industries, 50
aphorisms, xiv, xvn1; witticisms and, 36
Arabic, 9
art collection, 39
awards, 2

Bank of Nova Scotia (BNS), 84; Jamaica and, 89–96. *See also* Scotia Bank
banks, 84–85; government and, 89. *See also specific banks*
Barber, Horace, 78
Barclays Bank, 75
bauxite, 1, 2; Jamaica and, 76; production of, 75
benefactors, 40
BITU. *See* Bustamante Industrial Trade Union
BNS. *See* Bank of Nova Scotia

BPO. *See* business processing outsourcing
Brown, Dick, 95
bureaucracy, 31
business, xiii; conglomerate as, 49, 107; emigration and, 55; family and, 107; goals for, 24; Jamaica and, 111; management of, 55; predictions for, 31; skills and, 62; tire retreading as, 23
business processing outsourcing (BPO), 93
Bustamante, Alexander, 27, 70, 71, 72
Bustamante Industrial Trade Union (BITU), 72

Cable and Wireless (C&W), 91; profits for, 94
CAC. *See* Conditionedair and Associated Contractors
calculators, 43
capital, 24
career, 3
the Caribbean, 3, 10; history and, 107
Caribbean Metal Products (CMP), 30
Castel, Sara ("Sarita"), 34–36, *35*, *37*, 38–39, 79, 104–5
Chen, Lucien, 43
children, 38

cholera, 14
cigarettes, 39
Clarke, Bill, 90–91
class, 14, 36, 54; emergence and, 12
clothing, 19; standards and, 38
CMP. *See* Caribbean Metal Products
cocoa, 29
Colonial Bank (UK), 89
colonialism, 77; economy and, 30, 92; island nations and, 109
commerce, 12
Commodity Service Company Limited, 24–25, 49
Conditionedair and Associated Contractors (CAC), 50
construction, 59; precedents in, 61
context, 101; whiteness and, 26
contributions, 90; policy and, 105
Council of Economic Advisors, 4
cousins, 109
creditors, 16
crime, 53
Cuba, 9, 94
customer service, 25
C&W. *See* Cable and Wireless

Damascus, 10
Davies, Omar, 4, 82, 84–85; tribute by, 90
Davis, Carlton, 75–76
death, 1, 20, 104; of Henriques, 54; Matalon, Mayer, and, 105; of Newman, 46; siblings and, 57
debt, 57; reduction of, 100; subsidiaries and, 99
decision making, 71
deficit, 78
DeMercado, Barbara, 109
DeMercado, Marjorie, 109
Digicel, 96
discourse, 117; popular culture in, 63
distribution, 26; pharmaceuticals and, 27
diversification, 110
dry goods market, 11

Eagleburger, Lawrence ("Larry"), 76–77
Eagle Star Insurance, 61
economy, 26; colonialism and, 30, 92; contraction of, 111; Jamaica and, 49, 101; policy and, 28, 85; volatility and, 52
education, 16, 20, 74; elites and, 114; free education, 78; institutions and, 52; obsession with, 40
elections, 27; JLP and, 80; reassignments and, 95
elites: education and, 114; prejudice from, 32
emigration, 54; business and, 55; family and, 108
emotional intelligence, 33
employment, 19
Essays on Power & Change in Jamaica (Stone), 51
ethnography, 118
events, 10, 19; trauma and, 53
experience, 24; advice and, 28
exports, 29

facts, 107; trajectory and, 108
family, 6, 117; business and, 107; conflict and, 99, 109; dispersion and, 54, 109; emigration and, 108; generations and, 111; sacrifice for, 102. *See also* siblings
Fidanque, Nelson, 34
financial sector, 85; liberalization of, 101
fiscal profligacy, 78
flight, 32
floods, 16
foreign exchange market, 99
Foreshore Development Company, 46
Fullana Brothers, 59

gambling, 38; calculations and, 43; wins at, 44
GDP. *See* Gross Domestic Product
Gibraltar Camp, 14

Glass Slipper nightclub, 15
Glasspole, Florizel, *2*, 69, 72, 110
goals, 113; business and, 24
Golding, Bruce, 1, 86
Goodman, Jack, 23
Goodman, Pauline, 16, 19, 23–27, 29, 52, 54
government, 5; banks and, 89; concerns about, 77; housing and, 66; negotiations and, 75; networking with, 110; shareholders as, 92; telecommunications and, 93
grievances, 113
Gross Domestic Product (GDP), 30
guayaberas, 104
Guyana, 29

the *Hamburg* ship, 9
Hamilton, Howard, 83
health, 54
the Hebrew Benevolent Society, 14
Henriques, Florizel Madge, 11–16, 19, *35*, 35–36, *51*, 54; daughters-in-law of, 35
history, 74; the Caribbean and, 107; financial crisis in, 101; Jamaica and, 74, 118
holidays, 36
Home Appliances Finance Corporation, 50
honors, 90
horses, 38; knowledge of, 45; racing of, 44
Hosiery Company of Jamaica, 57
housing, 3, *60*, 107; developers and, 104; government and, 66; in Jamaica, 59, *60*; Trinidad and, 63; WIHCON and, 56
humor, xiv; as risqué, 36; teasing and, 39
Hurricane Gilbert, 86

ICD. *See* Industrial Commercial Development
ideas, 5; mechanisms for, 43

immigration, 13
IMP. *See* Institute of Management and Production
impact, xiii
imports, 29; competition and, 57; vehicles for, 50
Industrial Commercial Development (ICD), 3, 45, 103; success of, 112
industry, 76
inflation, 94
influence, xiii; loss of, 84, 96; opinion and, 34; policy and, 79; relationships and, 77
information technology, 95
infrastructure, 94
initial public offering (IPO), 100
Institute of Management and Production (IMP), 52
integrity, 6
investments, 30, 73, 81; opportunity for, 56
IPO. *See* initial public offering
Isaacs, Wills, 71
island nations, 113
Israel, 10, 14–15, 25, 34–36, 63, 81

Jamaica, xv; bauxite in, 76; BNS and, 89–96; business in, 111; economy and, 49, 101; exodus from, 54; families in, 117; fiscal deficit, 78; history and, 74, 118; housing in, 59, *60*; independence and, 73; industry in, 76; Jewish people in, 13; nationalism and, 70; power in, 51; stories about, 72
Jamaica Agro Products (JAP), 81
Jamaica College (JC), 1, 16; alumni of, 18
Jamaica Defence Force, 71
Jamaica Labour Party (JLP), 27; elections and, 80
Jamaican-Jewish community, 15, 79, 113; families from, 117
Jamaica Racehorse Owners' Association, 45

Jamaica Telephone Company (JTC), 80–81; leadership of, 91
JAP. *See* Jamaica Agro Products
JC. *See* Jamaica College
JLP. *See* Jamaica Labour Party
journalists, 72
JTC. *See* Jamaica Telephone Company

Knight, Franklyn, 63
knowledge, 31; of horses, 45

labor riots, 73
languages, 9; dialect and, 12
leadership, *62*; positions of, 1, 107; transitions and, 91
legacy, 20, 84; awareness of, 117
the Levant, 10
licenses, 52
lifestyle, 55
Liguanea Club, 32
listening, 33
Little Theatre Movement, 15
loans, 5; Scotia Bank and, 102. *See also* Bank of Nova Scotia
Longbridge, Gladys, 72
Lowry, L. S., 39

magnanimity, 3
Manley, Michael, xiii, 74–75, 77, 94, 107; associations with, 4, 18, 70, 73; biography of, 83; power and, 73; suggestions to, 66; support for, 80
Manley, Norman, xiii, 1, 18, 27, 59–60, 70, 72, 110; approvals by, 71; entourage of, 82
manufacturing, 30, 112
marketing, 60
marriage, 14, 35; brothers and, 109
Matalon, Aaron, 15–6, 19–20, 23, 25, 29, 32, 52, 54, 57, 100–102, 104; hold up of, 53; quotes by, 69
Matalon, Adele, 16, *51*, 52, 54

Matalon, Eli, 16, 19, 23, 29, 31, *35*, 39, *51*, 52, 54, 74, 78, 83, 110; office held by, 107
Matalon, Florizel. *See* Henriques, Florizel Madge
Matalon, Isaac, 15, 21n26
Matalon, Joseph, 9–16, 18–20, 108, 113
Matalon, Joseph A., 38, 100, 108
Matalon, Joseph M., 2, 15, 38, 56, 102, 105, 108, 119 *103*; tribute by, 6
Matalon, Leah, 16, 32, 52
Matalon, Mayer. *See specific topics*
Matalon, Moses, 16, 18, 20, 23, 32, 39, *51*, 54–57, 78, 107, 109, 110
Matalon, Owen, 16, 39, *51*, 52, 54, 56, 61–62, 65, 104
Matalon, Rebeca, xi, 38, 104
Matalon, Sarita. *See* Castel, Sara ("Sarita")
Matalon, Vernon, 16, 19, 32, 39, 45, *51*, 52, 54, 104
Matalon, Zackie, *51*, 54, 69–70, 107, 109, 112
Matalon and Company, 16; subsidiary as, 25
Matalon Malca, Jacqueline, xi, 38, 44
mathematics, 18; aptitude for, 43
McIntyre, Alister, 75
Mechala Investments, 99–100
mediation, 91
memory, 33
merchants, 11–12
Merrill Lynch, 100
Mexico, 65, 79
migration, 10, 54
Miller, Errald, 95–96
mining, 30
misperceptions, 64
mobile services, 96
models, 18; housing and, 59
Money Index, 108
monopoly, 94
mortgage financing, 61

Mountain, Brian, 61, 94
Murray, R. M. ("Reggie"), 18

National Commercial Bank, 75
National Housing Trust, 65–66, 75, 79, 105
nationalism, 70
National Workers' Union (NWU), 72
negotiations, 4, 102; government and, 75; independence and, 73; listening and, 33
Newman, Paul, 45, 46
nicknames, xiv; assignment of, 39–40
Nigeria, 63
NHT. *See* National Housing Trust
NWU. *See* National Workers' Union

Obasanjo, Olusegun, 63
opinion, 71, 79, 91; influence and, 34
opportunity, 23, 74; investment as, 56; offers and, 61; recognition of, 31
options, 12
Order of Jamaica, 2
outcome, 33
ownership, 84, 92

packaging, 29
paintings, 39
Panama, 9; life in, 104; Sephardim in, 34, 79; work in, 23
Patterson, P. J., 4, 38, 64, 82; memoir of, 83, 87n30
Paulwell, Phillip, 95
People's National Party (PNP), 27; resentment by, 78; support for, 69
personal life, 2; consolidation of, 34
Petroleum Corporation of Jamaica, 83
pharmaceuticals, 26–27
phenotypes, 26
philosophy, xiv
photographs, *17*, *24*, *92*, *103*; horse racing in, *44*; housing in, *60*; leadership in, *62*; siblings in, *51*; wedding in, *35*
Pickersgill, Robert ("Bobby"), 95

PNP. *See* People's National Party
poetry, 6; by Smith, 18–19
policy: contributions and, 105; economy and, 28, 85; errors and, 80; influence and, 79
politics: advice and, 86; business and, 31; relationships and, 74; siblings and, 69–70
popular culture: discourse in, 63; misperceptions in, 64; songs and, 15
population, 27, 109
portrayals, 113
ports, 65
the Portugals, 13
power, xiii; families in, 51; Manley, M., in, 73
pragmatism, 28, 49
prejudice, 32
Private Sector Organization of Jamaica (PSOJ), 3
privatization, 85; utilities and, 93
privilege, 109
profits, 40, 90; C&W and, 94; income and, 115
property, 38
PSOJ. *See* Private Sector Organization of Jamaica
publicity, xiv

quotes, 69; opportunity in, 23

race and color, 11; opportunity and, 74; privilege and, 109; society and, 13
railroad, 10
reading, 6
real estate, 57
recognition, xiv
Reid, Stanley, 51
relationships, 40, 71, 91; breach in, 79; influence of, 77; management of, 108; politics and, 74; shifts in, 82
religion, 13; practice of, 16
reputation, 61
retail, 50
revenues, 5

rice, 29
risk, 102
Rousseau, Pat, xi, 45–46, 61, 75, 101, 119; tribute by, 5–6

The San Jose Accord of 1980, 65
scandal, 109; cons and, 111
scarcity, 53
scholarships, 43, 90
Scotia Bank, 101; loan from, 102. *See also* Bank of Nova Scotia
Seaga, Edward, 46, 64, 70; plans by, 81
Sephardim, 9; in Panama, 34, 79
services, 94
Shalom, Felix, 34
shareholders: Matalon, Joseph, M., as, 103; siblings as, 55, 99
sharing, 25
Shearer, Hugh, *62*; introductions by, 86; message from, 73
Shell Oil, 82–83
siblings, xiv, 109; allocations for, 40; business and, 107; death of, 57; household and, 19; photographs with, *51*; politics and, 69–70; shareholders as, 55, 99
skills, 6, 33, 112; organization and, 62
Smith, M. G., 18–19
social entrepreneurship, xiii
social hierarchy, 26
social responsibility, 66
society, 11; hysteria in, 53; race and color in, 13
songs, 15, 64
speeches, 77
Spring Plains project, 81–82
stereotypes, 118
stock exchange, 50, *92*; IPO and, 100
Stone, Carl, 51
stories, 118
St. Thomas, 70
subsidiaries, 50; closing of, 57; debt and, 99; Matalon and Company as, 25; WIHCON as, 100

synagogue, 14; attendance at, 36
Syria, 10
the Syrians, 11–12

Tanna, Dhiru, 80–81
Tavares, Clem, 72
technology, 44, 95; capacity, 93
Telecommunications of Jamaica (TOJ), 46, 91, 93
textiles, 10
tire retreading, 23
Tisona, Eli, 81–82
TOJ. *See* Telecommunications of Jamaica
tourism, 30; UDC and, 65
travel, 38
Trinidad, 63
trust, 25
Turkish Ottoman Empire, 10
Turnball Farm, 45
Tyndall, Shirley, 5, 84

UDC. *See* Urban Development Corporation
United Congregation of Israelites, 1, 22n36; as director of, 36
United Congregation of Israelites School, 19
United States, 59, 109
unity, 20; breakdown of, 53
University of the West Indies, 52
University of the West Indies, Mona: honorary doctorate from, 3; scholarships to, 90
Urban Development Corporation (UDC), 45, 46n3; tourism and, 65
utilities, 93

values, 25
Venezuela, 65
Vybz Kartel, 64

wealth, 51, 56
weddings, *35*, *37*
Weller, Dell, 45

West Indies Home Contractors (WIHCON), 49; establishment of, 60; housing projects by, 56; subsidiary status of, 100
whiteness, 14; context and, 26

WIHCON. *See* West Indies Home Contractors
World War II, 20

Young, Lord David, 94–95

About the Author

Diana Thorburn is a Jamaican researcher, writer and editor. Born and raised in Jamaica, she is a graduate of the Johns Hopkins University School of Advanced International Studies. Formerly a lecturer at the University of the West Indies, Mona, she is presently the director of research at a Caribbean public policy think tank. This is her first nonacademic publication.

www.ingramcontent.com/pod-product-compliance
Lightning Source LLC
Chambersburg PA
CBHW070643300426
44111CB00013B/2235